SERIES EDITORS

TRACY L. PELLETT   JACK RUTHERFORD   CLAUDIA BLACKMAN

Skills, Drills & Strategies for

Volleyball

Tracy L. Pellett
Curt Lox

Routledge
Taylor & Francis Group

LONDON AND NEW YORK

Library of Congress Cataloging-in-Publication Data

Pellet, Tracy L.
    Skills , drills & stategies for volleyball / Tracy L. Pellet,
Curt Lox.
        p.   cm. — (The teach, coach, play series)
    Includes index.
    ISBN 1–890871–13–3
    1. Volleyball.   2. Volleyball—Training.   I. Lox, Curt.
II. Title.   III. Title: Skills, drills, and strategies for volleyball.   IV. Series.
GV1015.3.P455   2000
796.325—dc21   99–14472
                                                                                    CIP

First published 2000 by Holcomb Hathaway, Publishers, Inc.

Published 2017 by Routledge
2 Park Square, Milton Park, Abingdon, Oxon OX14 4RN
711 Third Avenue, New York, NY 10017, USA

Routledge is an imprint of the Taylor & Francis Group, an informa business

Copyright © 2000 by Taylor & Francis

All rights reserved. No part of this book may be reprinted or reproduced or utilised in any form or by any electronic, mechanical, or other means, now known or hereafter invented, including photocopying and recording, or in any information storage or retrieval system, without permission in writing from the publishers.

Notice:
Product or corporate names may be trademarks or registered trademarks, and are used only for identification and explanation without intent to infringe.

ISBN-13 978-1-890871-13-0 (pbk)

Contents

SECTION 3   **Skills and Drills**   **15**

SECTION 4   Strategies   49

SECTION 5   Glossary   61

About the Authors

Tracy L. Pellett is an Assistant Professor in the School of Education at the University of Arkansas-Monticello. After completing his bachelor's degree in physical education from Carthage College in Kenosha, Wisconsin and his master's degree from Ball State University in Muncie, Indiana, Dr. Pellet earned his Doctorate of Education from Brigham Young University.

Dr. Pellet was active in sports at the collegiate level and has coached a variety of sports in his career. He has a particular interest in volleyball and has published refereed articles regarding proper volleyball learning progression and equipment use in such journals as *Strategies,* the *Journal of Physical Education, Recreation and Dance,* the *Journal of Teaching in Physical Education,* and *Perceptual and Motor Skills.*

Dr. Pellett currently resides in Monticello, Arkansas, with his wife Heidi, son Avery, and daughter Abigail.

Curt Lox is an Associate Professor and Director of the Graduate Program in the Department of Kinesiology and Health Education at Southern Illinois University Edwardsville. Dr. Lox received his bachelor's degree in psychology from the University of California at Riverside, his master's degree in physical education and sport studies from Miami University, Ohio, and his doctorate in kinesiology from the University of Illinois at Urbana Champaign.

Dr. Lox has been involved in sports as a player, coach, and sport psychologist and currently serves as a consultant to a number of athletes and teams in the St. Louis area. He has authored over 20 scientific articles and book chapters related to the field of health, exercise, and sport psychology.

Dr. Lox currently resides in Edwardsville, Illinois, with his wife Shea and daughter Kelsey.

Preface

WELCOME TO THE *TEACH, COACH, PLAY* SERIES

The books in the *Teach, Coach, Play* series emphasize a systematic learning approach to sports and activities. Both visual and verbal information are presented so that you can easily understand the material and improve your performance.

Built-in learning aids help you master each skill in a step-by-step manner. Using the cues, summaries, skills, drills, and illustrations will help you build a solid foundation for safe and effective participation now and in the future.

This text is designed to illustrate correct techniques and demonstrate how to achieve optimal results. Take a few minutes to become familiar with the textbook's organization and features. Knowing what to expect and where to look for material will help you get the most out of the textbook, your practice time, and this course.

TO THE INSTRUCTOR

Your needs are changing, your courses are changing, your students are changing, and the demands from your administration are changing. By setting out to create a series of books that addresses many of these changes, we've created a series that:

- Provides complete, consistent coverage of each sport—the basics through skills and drills to game strategies so you can meet the needs of majors and non-majors alike.
- Includes teaching materials so that new and recently assigned instructors have the resources they need to teach the course.
- Allows you to cover exactly the sports and activities you want with the depth of coverage you want.

What's in the *Teach, Coach, Play* Series?

- Nine activities:

    Skills, Drills, & Strategies for Badminton
    Skills, Drills, & Strategies for Basketball
    Skills, Drills, & Strategies for Bowling
    Skills, Drills, & Strategies for Golf

Skills, Drills, & Strategies for Racquetball

Skills, Drills, & Strategies for Strength Training

Skills, Drills, & Strategies for Swimming

Skills, Drills, & Strategies for Tennis

Skills, Drills, & Strategies for Volleyball

■ Accompanying Instructor's Manuals

What's in the Student *Teach, Coach, Play* Textbooks?

The basic approach in all of the *Teach, Coach, Play* activity titles is to help students improve their skills and performance by building mastery from simple to complex levels.

The basic organization in each textbook is as follows:

Section 1 overviews history, organizations and publications, conditioning activities, safety, warm-up suggestions, and equipment.

Section 2 covers exercises or skills, participants, action involved, rules, facility or field, scoring, and etiquette.

Section 3 focuses on skills and drills or program design.

Section 4 addresses a broad range of strategies specifically designed to improve performance now and in the future.

Section 5 provides a convenient glossary of terms.

Supplements to Support You and Your Students

The *Teach, Coach, Play* books provide useful and practical instructional tools. Each activity is supported by its own manual. Each of these instructor's manuals includes classroom management notes, safety guidelines, teaching tips, ideas for inclusion of students with special needs, drills, lesson plans, evaluation notes, test bank, and a list of resources for you.

Preliminaries

Welcome to the world of volleyball, one of the fastest growing sports for males and females in the world! It is our goal to present the novice player with information concerning the fundamentals of volleyball, including the physical and mental skills needed to succeed and have fun. You will find that volleyball is a relatively easy sport to learn, is an ideal form of physical activity, and provides numerous opportunities to interact with others. Most importantly, volleyball is a sport that individuals of all ages can enjoy and one that may be played both indoors and outdoors, recreationally or competitively. Let us begin with a brief history of the game.

HISTORY, CURRENT STATUS, AND FUTURE OF VOLLEYBALL

The invention of volleyball dates back to 1895 and is generally credited to William Morgan, a YMCA physical education director in Holyoke, Massachusetts. Morgan originally developed **mintonette,** a game designed as a less strenuous alternative to the game of basketball. Mintonette utilized the bladder of a basketball and a badminton net set at a height of 6 feet 6 inches with the game progressing by innings as in baseball. The object of the game was to put the ball on the opponent's side of the floor using only the hands while, at the same time, preventing the ball from landing on your own side of the floor. Interestingly, no restrictions were placed on the participants in terms of the number of players on a side or the number of ball contacts allowed. Shortly thereafter, Morgan was influenced to change the name of the game to the more appropriate and appealing name of "volleyball."

From 1897 through the 1920s, official rules and equipment were introduced to the sport. The Spalding Company created the first volleyball, the net was raised to 7 feet, and the YMCA assumed the role of promoter for the sport. Later, rotating positions were specified and the net was raised to 7 feet 6 inches (and later to 8 feet). An official volleyball game consisted of the first team to twenty-one points (later changed to fifteen points) and a match consisted of the first team to win two games. Scholastic programs were developed and national championships were played. In addition, rules that restricted the ball to be contacted above the waist and no more than three times per side were introduced, and court dimensions were set at 35 feet wide and 60 feet long. Finally, the **United States of America Volleyball Association (USAV)** and the first collegiate volleyball team, at Oregon State College, were formed.

mintonette original name of the game known as volleyball

United States of America Volleyball Association (USAV) governing body for the sport of volleyball in the United States

Federation Internationale de Volleyball (FIVB) *governing body for amateur international volleyball*

The 1940s through 1960s brought specificity to the game in terms of positions as well as the 3–3 and 4–2 offensive formations, which provided for more complex and organized systems of movement strategy. Of major importance, the United States armed forces played volleyball recreationally and are probably most responsible for introducing the sport to the rest of the world. To this end, the **Federation Internationale de Volleyball (FIVB),** the governing body of amateur international volleyball, was organized in 1947, and females were finally welcomed to the game in 1949. Opportunities for children and full-time coaches also emerged at this time, and in 1964, volleyball became an Olympic sport for both men and women, thus paving the way for successful international competitions that continue to thrive today.

Currently, the sport of volleyball is growing by leaps and bounds in the United States and throughout the world. In fact, volleyball is the leading competitive sport in approximately half of the countries in which it is played. The televising of collegiate, professional (including beach volleyball), and international competitions, in concert with the growing emphasis on the game in recreational and scholastic settings, has led to a surge in popularity of volleyball not likely to be dampened in the near future. The game is no longer played solely by businessmen content with lobbing the ball back and forth over the net as was the case in the game's early stages of development. Indeed, the power and intensity that characterize the current state of competitive volleyball are testament to the progressive change that has taken place since its inception over 100 years ago.

ORGANIZATIONS ASSOCIATED WITH VOLLEYBALL

The primary governing body for volleyball in the United States is the United States of America Volleyball (USAV) Association. The USAV provides the rules and standards for competitive games and produces publications, videos, and clinics. In addition, information about youth, club, and Olympic volleyball, as well as coaching education, may be found here. For more information, contact the USAV at the following address or phone number:

United States of America Volleyball (USAV)
3595 East Fountain Boulevard, Suites 1–2
Colorado Springs, CO 80910–1740
(800) 275-8782

For information concerning the sport of volleyball on an international level, write to the following:

Federation Internationale de Volleyball (FIVB)
Avenue de la Gare 12
Ch-1003 Lausanne
Switzerland

For information regarding girls' interscholastic or women's intercollegiate volleyball, contact the following organization:

National Association of Girls and Women in Sports (NAGWS)
1900 Association Drive
Reston, VA 22091–1599
(800) 321-0789

Boys' and girls' interscholastic (high school) sports, including volleyball, are governed by the National Federation of State High School Associations (NFSHSA). They may be contacted at the following address:

National Federation of State High School Associations (NFSHSA)
11724 Plaza Circle
P.O. Box 20626
Kansas City, MO 64195

Men's and women's intercollegiate (college/university) sports, including volleyball, are governed by one of three bodies, depending on the level of competition. They are as follows:

National Collegiate Athletic Association (NCAA)
Nall Avenue at 63rd Street
P.O. Box 1906
Mission, KS 66201

National Association for Intercollegiate Athletics (NAIA)
1221 Baltimore
Kansas City, MO 64105

National Junior College Athletic Association (NJCAA)
P.O. Box 7305
Colorado Springs, CO 80933

VOLLEYBALL PUBLICATIONS

Numerous magazines, books, and videos targeting all skill levels in volleyball are readily available for players and coaches, including a complete line of publications available through Volleyball Informational Products (VIP). VIP is a joint educational venture formed by the USAV and the American Volleyball Coaches Association (AVCA). The company may be contacted at the following address:

Volleyball Informational Products
1227 Lake Plaza Drive, Suite B
Colorado Springs, CO 80906
Phone: (800) 275–8782
Fax: (719) 576–7778

The following is a short list and description of some of the products available through VIP.

SELECTED VIDEOS

Serving and Serve Strategy
Author: Terry Pettit
39 minutes
Description: Explains how serve is a unique, fundamental skill. The mechanics of the floater, top spin and jump serves are explained, with attention given to special serving problems, the serving roles for players, the identification of serving zones, and individual serving strategies.

Team Drills
Author: John Dunning
48 minutes
Description: Explains and demonstrates drills for working on team and individual skills. It discusses the philosophy behind the drills and their progression from easy to hard. The video also provides important keys to remember when running the drills.

Team Offensive Systems
Author: Vicki Mealer
34 minutes
Description: Explains and demonstrates the 4–2, international 4–2, 6–2, and 5–1 offensive systems. It also demonstrates the four- and five- person serve receive patterns and variations in receiving alignment.

SELECTED BOOKS

Coaches Guide to Beginning Volleyball Programs
Author: VIP Publications
Emphasis for beginning coaches and youth programs. Lesson plans, skill and drill development, youth games and variations, motor skill highlights.

Rookie Coaches Guide
Author: VIP Publications
Written and designed for the complete novice. Provides the new coach with the basic fundamental skills, techniques, and strategies.

(continued)

The Best of Coaching Volleyball Book I
Author: VIP Publications
A beginner level publication geared to teaching the basics of the game of volleyball, from establishing a solid volleyball program to instructing players. In addition, a number of applicable drills are offered.

The Best of Coaching Volleyball Book II: Advanced Elements of the Game
Author: VIP Publications
An advanced level publication geared to teaching the more advanced elements of the game from defense and attack to blocking, serving, and serve reception. In addition, a number of applicable drills are offered.

OTHER RESOURCES

The following are periodicals that might be helpful in learning more about the game of volleyball.

Periodicals
Coaching Volleyball
1227 Lake Plaza Dr.
Suite B
Colorado Springs, CO 80906
This periodical is the official technical journal of the American Volleyball Coaches Association. It is published six times a year with an annual subscription rate of $20.00.

Scholastic Coach
50 West 44 St.
New York, NY 10036
This periodical contains several helpful coaching articles regarding a variety of sports such as volleyball. It is published monthly from August to May/June with an annual subscription rate of $20.00.

CONDITIONING

aerobic exercise a form of training/conditioning that utilizes oxygen in order to produce energy needed for long-duration activity

anaerobic exercise a form of training/conditioning that does not require oxygen utilization to produce energy needed for short-duration bursts of activity

range of motion flexibility/mobility of a joint

General Conditioning

As volleyball is an activity that requires both short bursts of power and moderate levels of cardiovascular endurance, both **aerobic exercise** and **anaerobic exercise** training must be included in any volleyball conditioning program. Flexibility exercises, which serve to increase **range of motion** and warm up muscles such that they do not tear or strain, should also be incorporated into the training regimen (see the section on "Warming Up for Volleyball"). Stretching should proceed in a *slow* manner, without bouncing, prior to all games and practices. Particular attention should be given to proper stretching of muscles in the back and legs as these are the primary muscles used in the sport of volleyball.

Weight Training

Weight training is one form of anaerobic conditioning that can be of great value to volleyball enthusiasts. A proper weight training regimen, consisting of any combination of free weights and universal weight training machines, should be used for increasing muscular strength and endurance. Specifically, exercises that target the back and legs should be incorporated in order to delay muscle fatigue and increase the power needed to perform the various skills required in volleyball. Examples of such exercises include squats, leg presses, and leg extensions for the quadricep muscles (thigh), leg curls for the hamstrings (upper back leg), and toe raises for the calf muscles (lower back leg). Back machines, as well as exercises that utilize one's own body weight, can be utilized to strengthen back muscles.

Plyometrics

Plyometrics ("box jumping") is another anaerobic exercise that can be used in place of or along with the above weight training exercises. With plyometrics, the individual jumps off a platform (anywhere from 1 foot to 3 feet high) and lands simultaneously with both feet on the ground. The knees bend to absorb the shock of the landing, and the muscles of the legs contract like the pulling back of a rubber band. Following the contraction, the individual explodes into another jump (either straight up or forward) utilizing the rebound effect of the contracted muscles, similar to letting go of the rubber band. Prolonged training in this fashion serves to increase the elasticity of the leg muscles, thereby improving one's jumping ability. Proper training from a knowledgeable coach or fitness trainer is needed, however, in order to prevent foot, ankle, or achilles tendon injuries.

Aerobic Exercise

Aerobic exercise, used to train for cardiovascular endurance or stamina, may be accomplished via numerous examples of traditional exercise and modern technology. Jogging, running, or bicycling for a period of at least 15 to 20 consecutive minutes have traditionally been the activities of choice. However, treadmills, stairclimbers, stationary bicycles, rowers, and simulated cross-country ski machines may also be used as indoor alternatives. **Interval training,** an aerobic training program that also consists of an anaerobic component, is probably the ideal program for the sport of volleyball. In interval training, the individual performs the exercise in an intermittent manner using a preestablished pattern of work and rest intervals. As an example, one might sprint for a period of 10 seconds, rest for 5 seconds, sprint for 10 seconds, and so forth for a specified period of time. The benefit of this form of exercise is that one can train for endurance, and explosive short-term power at the same time. Combining this mode of exercise with appropriate weight training, flexibility, and jumping exercises would produce an extremely comprehensive training regimen.

interval training *a conditioning program that trains both the aerobic and anaerobic energy systems by utilizing a pattern of work and rest intervals*

Specific Conditioning

Conditioning exercises specific to the skills used in volleyball should be utilized in addition to the general conditioning exercises discussed previously. Context-specific activities not only help the body to become physically conditioned, but also develop skills that are directly related to successful play. Several popular and effective volleyball-specific exercises are listed below.

■ Partner Net Jump

Partners of the same height are placed on opposite sides of the net facing one another and proceed to slide sideways two strides along the length of the net, at which point the partners jump and clap each other's hands above the net. The process can be repeated for a certain length of time or for a certain number of jumps.

■ Blocking Cycle

This exercise builds off of the partner net jump in that one blocker moves along the net and blocks the left, middle, and right spikers, in order. A setter delivers the ball to the next spiker just as the blocker has completed the jump against the previous spiker. The process can be repeated for a predetermined number of cycles.

■ Simulated Spiking

Players jump and simulate the spiking action using the standard approach and takeoff. The process may be repeated twenty to thirty times with little or no rest in between jumps to train technique, endurance, and power at the same time.

■ **Spiking Cycle**

This exercise builds off of simulated spiking in that the spiker performs a continuous number of spikes incorporating a volleyball, setter, and teammates to aid in retrieving the balls.

■ **Setting Cycle**

Three setters line up approximately 10 feet apart along the length of the net and jump-set the ball to one another in order, with the setter in the middle always back-setting the ball. The setter at the end of the cycle can either set it back to the middle or across the court to the setter who initiated the cycle.

■ **Forearm Passing Cycle**

Players start at one end of the back line and proceed to run down the line to forearm pass a toss or spike hit from the net. Following the pass, the players continue on to the other end of the back line and the cycle is repeated for a set number of passes.

Safety Notes

a. Use elbow and knee pads to avoid pain and injury when diving onto the floor.
b. Always warm up and cool down to avoid injuries, cramping, and soreness.
c. Inspect the playing surface, equipment, and apparel to ensure that hazards such as a wet floor, slick shoes, or jewelry will not lead to injury.
d. Do not wear a hat or baseball cap as the hat can fall off the head during play and pose a tripping hazard for you or your teammates.
e. Never serve until all teammates on the court are facing the net.

WARMING UP FOR VOLLEYBALL

Prior to participating in any vigorous activity, including volleyball, one should spend at least 5 to 10 minutes warming up. A proper warm-up serves to gradually increase heart rate, enhance flexibility, and mentally prepare the athlete for competition. Volleyball players should begin with a complete stretching regimen consisting of the following movements:

■ **Head Circles**

While standing, slowly move your head in as large a circle as possible (the motion of your head should resemble a halo). Gradually move your head in different directions by lowering it to touch your chest and shifting it from one shoulder to another. Be certain to rotate the head in both the clockwise and counterclockwise directions. Be cautious if attempting to move the head in a backward direction as this movement, if done haphazardly, can lead to injury.

■ **Trunk Reach and Stretch**

While standing with arms extended and hands joined above the head, slowly bend at the waist to the right or left. Hands and arms should reach to the side while the rest of the body continues to face forward. Hold the position for 5 to 10 seconds and then move to the other side. This stretch can also be done in a forward and backward position.

■ **Arm Circles**

While standing with both arms extended out to the side and parallel with the floor, slowly move arms in a circular motion making as large a circle with each arm as possible (i.e., the motion should look like a circle to someone looking at you from the side). Rotate arms ten times in both a clockwise and counterclockwise motion.

■ **Spike Stretch**

While standing, reach your spiking arm back behind your head with your fingers pointing down and your palm facing your back. Reach up with your opposite hand (palm facing away from your back) and lock fingers. Hold for 5 to 10 seconds and switch arms. Repeat two to three times.

■ **Groin Stretch**

While sitting with legs extended, gradually spread legs out beyond shoulder width as far as possible, pausing for 5 to 10 seconds. Continue on until you cannot spread legs wider without experiencing discomfort. Alternatively, sit with the bottom of your feet touching one another and knees out to the side while gradually bringing the feet in closer to the body.

■ **Leg Stretch**

While sitting with legs spread apart as in the groin stretch and toes pointed upward, reach forward toward one leg with both hands and grasp foot (or ankle, if necessary). Move your head toward your leg such that the forehead (if possible) touches the knee. Hold for 10 seconds and move to other leg. Repeat two to three times. Alternatively, stand with legs together and knees only slightly bent while bending over and touching the feet (or ankles, if necessary) with both hands. Hold for 10 seconds and repeat two to three times.

■ **Ankle Circles**

While sitting with legs extended straight out in front of you and raised off the floor, slowly rotate ankles in a circular motion, moving the feet in as large a circle as possible. Rotate feet 10 times in both a clockwise and counterclockwise motion.

Following the stretching exercises, players can engage in a number of warm-up movements, including the following:

■ **Jogging/Running**

Players can jog around the perimeter of the court and then run court sprints in which the pace (speed) of the running gradually increases.

■ **Rope Jumping**

Like jogging or running, jumping rope is a traditional favorite and an excellent warm-up exercise.

■ **Partner Ball Exchange**

Two players (one with a ball) stand back-to-back approximately 3 feet apart and turn, at the same time, to their right and exchange the ball. They then turn to the left and exchange the ball again. The process continues for a period of 30 to 60 seconds. Alternatively, players can exchange the ball by bending forward and passing the ball between their legs, followed by a return to the standing position whereby they then reach above and behind their heads to exchange the ball. Finally, players may stand facing each other on either side of the net and exchange the ball with hands extended above the net using simultaneous jumps. Players should land on both feet and immediately jump back into position for the next exchange. The process continues for 30 to 60 seconds.

■ Partner Net Jump

As mentioned earlier, partners may simulate blocking via the net jump. Half of the players line up single file on one side of the net and the other half line up on the opposite side with both sides facing one another and both lines on one of the sidelines. The first player in each line approaches the net, jumps, and claps the hands of the other above the net in a blocking motion. Players land on two feet, slide two steps toward the opposite side-line, and repeat the blocking motion. The process continues until the players reach the end of the net. Similar warm-ups can be done with mock spiking movements.

■ Pepper

Partners work on defense (dig), passing (set), and attacking (spike) by alternating these movements in a controlled fashion. Play begins when one player sets the ball to the other, who spikes the ball back to the setter. The setter then digs the ball back to the spiker, who then sets the ball, and the process continues.

EQUIPMENT   Footwear

Any court shoe will do (i.e., tennis, basketball), although volleyball-specific shoes are available. Running shoes are *not* acceptable as they have poor lateral (side-to-side) support and will leave black scuff marks on an indoor floor. All shoe heights (low-, mid-, and high-top), offering various degrees of ankle support, are acceptable. Cotton athletic socks should also be worn in order to pad and reduce stress on the feet, absorb sweat, reduce odor, and avoid blisters.

Clothing

Shorts and a T-shirt are appropriate apparel for volleyball (some players prefer long-sleeved T-shirts to ease the pain experienced from floor burns and contacting the ball many times in succession). Head and arm sweatbands and hair accessories may be used in order to keep sweat and hair out of the eyes. Hats are not recommended as they may pose a safety hazard.

Protective Gear

Knee and elbow pads come in a variety of shapes and sizes (and colors!) and are generally made of a hardened foam or rubber core and a soft elastic cover. All pads should fit snug, but not so much so that they become uncomfortable. Pads greatly reduce the discomfort sometimes experienced when the body meets the floor.

Volleyballs

Balls are generally white in color and consist of several pieces of leather or vinyl material that are sewn together. Standard (size #5) balls are 25 to 27 inches in circumference and weigh 9 to 10 ounces. Air pressure is maintained between 5.5 and 6.5 pounds per square inch (PSI). Modified volleyballs, which may be as much as 25 to 40 percent lighter, softer, and bigger, have been introduced on a large scale to aid beginners in developing skills and to remove the sting associated with the use of regulation balls.

Net

The net is 39 inches wide and 32 feet long and composed of a mesh material divided into 4-inch squares. A cable runs along the top of the net and a cord runs along the bottom of the net to keep it tight. Generally, the net is placed at a height of just over 7 feet 4 inches for women and just under 8 feet for men.

The Game

A brief introduction to the game of volleyball is presented in this section. Specifically, we will discuss (a) the mental and physical skills involved in volleyball, (b) the number of participants and their role in a game of volleyball, and (c) the basic action involved in volleyball.

Skills Involved in Volleyball

The object of the game of volleyball is to send the ball over the net such that the opposing team cannot return it without committing an error. In order to be successful, several physical and mental skills are necessary. Footwork skills are vital for optimal quickness and agility in volleyball and are particularly important for properly positioning oneself on the court. Jumping and eye-hand coordination are used extensively in many facets of the game. Mentally, the game requires anticipation, concentration, and excellent reflexes (reaction skills) as the ball and play often move at very rapid rates.

In terms of volleyball-specific skills, several actions are necessary. To direct a ball arriving at or below the waist to a teammate, the forearm pass should be used. To direct a ball to a teammate responsible for sending the ball over the net, or to receive a ball above the shoulders, players should perform the overhead pass or set. The spike is used by the offensive team to end play by forcibly hitting the ball downward toward the floor in the opposing team's court. The performance of the spike is generally reserved for two of the frontcourt players called the spikers, hitters, or attackers. To prevent or slow down a spiked ball at the net, the block is utilized. The block may only be performed by the frontcourt player(s). The final skill is the serve, which may be performed underhand or overhand. It is much like a pitched ball in baseball in that it is utilized to put the ball into play.

Participants and Teams

Although the number of participants can be modified, volleyball is generally played by two teams, with each team consisting of six players on the floor at a time (see Figure 2.1). These players include three frontcourt players, or forwards (left,

Figure 2.1

Diagram of volleyball court.

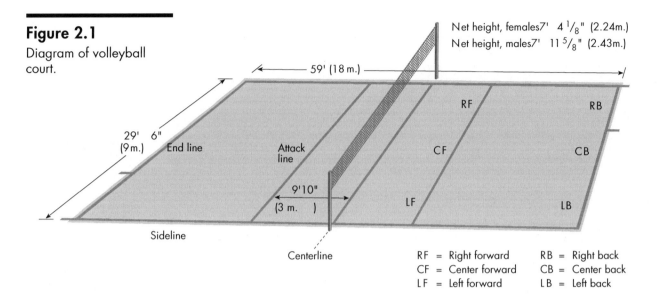

Net height, females 7' 4 ¹/₈" (2.24m.)
Net height, males 7' 11 ⁵/₈" (2.43m.)

59' (18 m.)

29' 6" (9 m.)   End line

Attack line

9'10" (3 m.)

Sideline

Centerline

RF   RB
CF   CB
LF   LB

RF = Right forward   RB = Right back
CF = Center forward   CB = Center back
LF = Left forward   LB = Left back

center, and right), and three backcourt players, or backs (left, center, and right). Typically, a competitive team is limited to twelve or fewer players, with the non-starters serving as substitutes. Two-on-two and three-on-three competitions are also popular, especially on the beach volleyball circuit.

Game Action

rally the action initiated with the serve and ending with a point or side-out

A coin-toss determines which team will serve and which side of the court each team will occupy for the first game. The ball is put into play by the right back player of the serving team from within the service area, and the **rally** begins once the receiving team makes contact and attempts to return the ball back over the net. The remaining players on the serving team must be within their respective playing areas during the serve (see Figure 2.1). Each team is allowed up to three consecutive contacts with the ball each time it is served or returned over the net by the opposing team. Although the goal of each possession is generally to convert a successful pass-set-spike sequence, it is permissible to return the ball back over the net after one or two contacts (a block is *not* considered a contact). Nonetheless, the first contact after the serve is generally a forearm pass. The purpose of this skill is to direct the ball to the frontcourt area to a teammate responsible for setting the ball. The set is then used to allow a teammate to spike the ball such that the other team will be unable to return it (called a **kill**). When an offensive player attempts a spike, the defensive team will generally attempt to block the **attack** in order to prevent the ball from crossing over into the defensive team's court. A point is scored only by the serving team and only when the receiving team fails to legally return the ball into the serving team's court. Thus, it is important for the receiving team to win each rally so that it may gain the right to serve (called a **side-out**) and prevent the serving team from scoring. Following a side-out only, and just prior to the serve, each player on the serving team rotates clockwise one position. Teams change sides after each game and at the middle of the third game as soon as one team reaches eight points.

kill a spike that cannot be returned

attack an offensive action intended to end play by hitting the ball to the floor on the opposing team's side of the court

side-out the result of the receiving team winning a rally; no points are scored

BASIC RULES AND VIOLATIONS

When serving, the ball must be tossed or released from the holding hand (nonhitting hand) and struck with either an open or closed hand such that the ball is sent over the net and into the opponent's court. While the ball is in play, the ball must be legally hit with the fingertips, open hand, or fist and may not be lifted, carried, or thrown. The ball cannot be contacted by any part of the body below the waist and a player may not contact the ball two consecutive times. A player contacting the ball while blocking, however, may make the next ball contact if the ball remains on the player's side of the net.

Players must be lined up on the court in their proper positions prior to the serve but may switch positions after the ball is put into play. A back-row player is not allowed to block or spike at the net but may, however, spike the ball if the take-off for the spike is behind the **attack line.**

Following a side-out, the team about to serve must **rotate** each player clock-wise one position. The player in the right front position rotates to the right back position and becomes the server. Serving out of turn results in a side-out for the opposing team and a cancellation of any points scored by the serving team.

During game action, a player may reach over the net but may not contact the ball over the net until the completion of the opponent's attack. The hand(s) may pass over the net during the follow-through after an attack and during blocking immediately following an attack by an opposing player. At no time may any part of the body of any player contact the net.

The ball may be played off of the net by either team except in the instance where one team has already made three contacts and the ball still resides on that team's side of the court. A served ball that contacts the net, goes under the net, or lands outside the net is considered "out" and results in a side-out for the receiving team. A ball struck by one team that lands outside the opposing team's court and that is not touched by that team is considered "out" and results in either a point or side-out for the team that originally struck the ball. However, a ball landing on any line that marks the boundary of the court is considered "in." A player may reach under the net or go outside of the court boundaries to play a ball on his or her side of the court. However, interfering with a player from an opposing team is illegal and results in a point or side-out for the opposing team.

Teams involved in competitive play are allowed two 30-second timeouts per game and a 3-minute rest period between games. A substitute may enter the game for any player on the team but must take the position of that player. Any player reentering the game must assume the original position in relation to his or her teammates. Any substitute who reenters the game must replace the same player he or she substituted for previously. Each team is limited to a total of twelve substitutions per game, and any one player is limited to three substitutions or entries per game (starting in a game is equivalent to one entry).

attack line a line on the court parallel to the net and located 9 feet 10 inches from either side of the center line; backcourt players must begin any attack from behind this line

rotation clockwise movement of players on the serving team just prior to a serve and immediately following a side-out

COURT DIMENSIONS AND MARKINGS

The typical indoor volleyball court is on a hardwood floor and measures 59 feet long and 29 feet 6 inches wide. The attack line is placed 9 feet 10 inches from the centerline, and the service area is measured 9 feet 10 inches from the right sideline and a minimum of 8 inches beyond the end line (see Figure 2.1).

SCORING

A match generally consists of the best of three games (i.e., the first team to win two games wins the match). Points can only be scored by the serving team. If the receiving team fails to return the ball legally over the net, the serving team scores a point and continues to serve. If the serving team makes an error on the serve or fails to correctly play a ball returned by the opposing team, the opposing team gains the right to serve (side-out). In standard scoring, the first team to score 15 points wins the game as long as the opposing team does not have 14 points. If this occurs, the teams continue to play until one team gains a lead of two points. Vol-

rally scoring   *a method of scoring in which a point is awarded when either the serving or receiving team wins the rally*

leyball may also be played according to a **rally scoring** method, whereby a point is awarded when either the serving or receiving team wins the rally. The team that wins the point serves next. Finally, games may be played for a specified amount of time using either standard or rally scoring. The winning team is that which is ahead when time expires.

ETIQUETTE

In general, most areas of etiquette are formally included in the game rules. These rules extend to player conduct, which is tightly monitored in the sport of volleyball. Numerous rules exist that penalize players for various forms of unsportsmanlike behavior, such as "trash talking" to an opponent or even speaking with an official. In volleyball, only the team captain may speak with an official, and generally this privilege is reserved for rule interpretation. Swearing, screaming, or displaying anger in any way may also be considered a conduct violation. These rules hold especially true for coaches and other bench personnel.

In many instances, games are played without officials, and players must make their own calls requiring honesty, discretion, and moral or ethical values. Rules for replays exist and may be used when opponents cannot come to a unanimous decision on a call. Several unwritten rules exist in the game of volleyball as well, particularly in less competitive settings. Examples include allowing your opponent to get into position and announcing the score before serving, and rolling the ball under the net in between changes in service.

Skills and Drills

The basic objective in playing volleyball is to try and hit the ball to the opponent's side of the court in such a way as to prevent the opponent from returning the ball. The best way for players to accomplish this objective is by developing several fundamental skills. Two preliminary skills, footwork and proper positioning, are important skills to master prior to engaging in other skills. *Serving* is an especially important skill to master as it is the only time during the game that your team can earn points. A good serve immediately puts the other team on the defensive and makes it difficult for them to establish any sort of offense. Thus, consistency in execution is critical. The *forearm pass* is another important skill to master as it allows players to contact balls waist level or lower. It is also used more often than any other skill in a volleyball game. The *overhead pass* or *set* is another important skill as it allows players to receive balls higher than shoulder level. This skill also sets up a strong offensive attack. The *spike* is probably the most powerful shot in volleyball and is important to learn because it can quickly end play. The *block* is fundamental since it is a team's first line of defense against another team's spike. If a player hopes to be well rounded and successful, it is imperative that he or she master each of the skills listed. It is also important that players be able to use the skills in combination with one another and to apply them in various game contexts. The rest of this section is designed to help players develop all of these skills through drills and games. Several more advanced skills are discussed at the end of this section.

Preview

Volleyball can be a very fast moving and dynamic game. This can make the game fun to watch but very difficult to perform. Movements must be efficient, accurate, and appropriately timed with a moving ball. The best way to accomplish this task is to make sure the hitter is ready to move in a variety of directions and to get his or her body to the best position to perform whatever skill is being attempted. Table 3.1 provides a short summary of the preliminary skills necessary to be a successful volleyball player.

PRELIMINARY SKILLS

TABLE 3.1	Preliminary skills.	
SKILL	**USES**	**IMPORTANCE**
Ready Position	Waiting position that should be used prior to executing most skills. This position allows movement in any direction.	This position allows a player to move quickly from one point on the court to another in any direction. Players are better able to perform a skill correctly when their bodies are prepared to move and perform.
Footwork	Forward, backward, and lateral movements that allow a player to maneuver quickly into position to execute a skill.	Proper footwork prepares a player to hit the ball in the most advantageous position.

ready position an anticipatory position that will allow players to move quickly in any direction

The **ready position** is an anticipatory position that will allow players to move in any direction very quickly. The ready position is the first actual skill presented for the developing player and is the foundation for all other skills. Table 3.2 provides a summary of the form characteristics or "cues" important for the proper execution of the ready position. This table also provides possible errors and causes of these errors. Figure 3.1 provides a visual representation of a properly performed ready position.

Figure 3.1
The ready position.

TABLE 3.2 Ready position: Cues, errors, and causes.

SKILL	CUES	COMMON ERRORS	CAUSES OF ERRORS
Ready Position	■ Feet shoulder-width apart ■ Knees bent with weight on balls of feet ■ Back straight with hands in front of body ■ Head up; focused on incoming ball	Falling off-balance Moving too slowly out of position Mistiming the movement	Feet too close together Not on balls of feet Not focusing eyes on the ball

Proper **footwork** is important in allowing a player to move around the court efficiently and effectively. Players have a limited time to react to balls that are hit over the net onto their side of the court. Thus, it is imperative that players be able to move forward, backward, and laterally (i.e., side to side) with ease. Table 3.3 provides a summary of the form characteristics or "cues" important for moving in these various directions, possible errors, and causes of these errors.

footwork ability to move forward, backward, and laterally with ease to react to volleyball

TABLE 3.3 Footwork: Cues, errors, and causes.

SKILL	CUES	COMMON ERRORS	CAUSES OF ERRORS
Forward Movement	■ Feet staggered with wide base ■ Knees bent and in front of feet ■ Shoulders in front of knees with hands in front of body ■ Head up and body focused in direction of movement	Falling off-balance Moving too slowly Running into teammate	Feet too close with narrow base Body too straight Head is not up
Backward Movement	■ Body low with feet staggered and wide base ■ Knees bent with weight on balls of feet ■ Shoulders in front of knees with hands in front of body ■ Head up and the front of body focused in direction of net	Falling backward on bottom	High body posture
Lateral Movement	■ Body low with feet side-by-side and wide base ■ Knees bent and in front of feet ■ Shoulderns in front of knees with hands in front of body ■ Feet sliding in direction of movement	Tripping while moving	Feet crossing during movement instead of sliding

SKILL 1 — Ready Position and Footwork

The following drills are designed to improve readiness and ability to move to any location of the court in a short time. It is recommended that these drills be used as a warm up to the introduction of other skills and later be combined with the actual execution of other skills to be most effective.

Follow the Leader Drill

A leader stands near the net facing the other players who are spread out on the court. Players begin in a ready position and follow either the verbal commands or actual movements of the leader. The leader can move backward, forward, or laterally in any direction (see Figure 3.2).

Line Run Drill

Players are lined up at end line and left sideline. On the "go" command, players begin sprinting to attack line, then move laterally to the right of the court until they get to the center. At this point, players move forward to the net and laterally (i.e., sliding) to the right until they reach the right sideline. Players then move backward to the end line, laterally to the left, and back to the starting point (see Figure 3.3). It should be noted that players are always facing the net during movement.

OPTIONS:
1. Gradually increase the number of times players complete the drill to make it more difficult.

Figure 3.2 (on left)
Movement of leader and hitter in "Follow the Leader" drill.

Figure 3.3 (on right)
Movement pattern in "Line Run" drill.

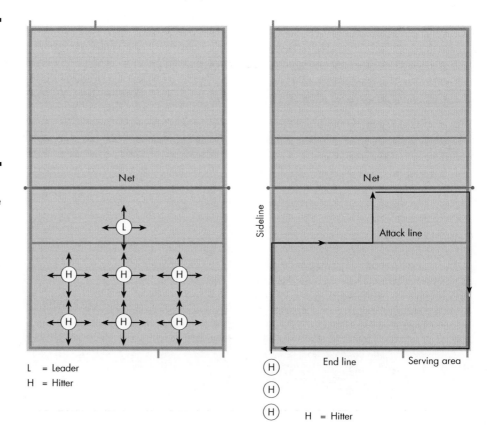

L = Leader
H = Hitter

H = Hitter

2. Reverse the direction of the pathway after all players have finished to make drill more interesting.

3. Have players pause at each point in the drill where there is a change in direction. Then have them demonstrate a good ready position, perform an exercise, or actually perform a skill.

Preview

The **forearm pass** or "bump" is probably one of the most important skills in volleyball to master as this skill is used more than any other skill in the game. The forearm pass is used to contact any ball below waist level with the forearms in an underhand manner. Generally, the forearm pass is the first contact made after the serve, and its purpose is to transfer the ball from the back to the front court (near the net) for another player to set or spike the ball. The forearm pass is the cornerstone for successful offensive play. Table 3.4 provides a short summary of the use of the forearm pass and its necessity in becoming a successful volleyball player. Table 3.5 provides a summary of the form characteristics or "cues" important for the proper execution of the forearm pass. This table also provides possible errors and causes of these errors. Figure 3.4 provides a visual representation of a properly performed forearm pass.

FOREARM PASS

forearm pass used to contact any ball below waist level (i.e., from a spike, the net, a block, or another forearm pass) with the forearms in an underhand manner

TABLE 3.4 Forearm pass.

SKILL	USES	IMPORTANCE
Forearm Pass	Contact balls that are waist high or lower (i.e., from a serve, a spike, the net, a block, or another forearm pass).	Allows the receiver more time to follow the ball before playing it. Allows for the handling of balls that have been hit hard.

TABLE 3.5 Forearm pass cues/errors/causes.

SKILL	CUES	COMMON ERRORS	CAUSES OF ERRORS
Forearm Pass	■ Body moves to get under ball and in-line with target. ■ Hands are together/arms straight. ■ Ball is contacted on forearms. ■ Arms stay lower than shoulders throughout hit. ■ Lift is from hips and legs. ■ Eyes stay focused on ball.	Player mistimes the movement. Ball travels directly upward or behind player after contact. Ball travels in direction other than what was intended.	Eyes are not focused on the ball. Player is not getting under ball because of poor footwork or ready position. Arms are swinging or being placed above shoulder height. Body is not facing target. Ball contacts hand.

Figure 3.4
A properly performed forearm pass.

| a   Ready | b   Performance | c   Follow-through |

The forearm pass is accomplished by clasping the hands together with the elbows straight and rotated inward in order to provide a flat, soft surface extending from the base of the wrists to the elbows. Once a player has positioned himself or herself under the ball, it is contacted in front of and to the center of the body. The ball should bounce off the low part of the forearms near the wrists. Since a slight lifting motion is needed by the legs as the ball is contacted, the knees must be bent and the back straight prior to contacting the ball. The greater the speed of the ball as it contacted, the less lift needed. It is paramount that the player keep his or her eyes focused on the ball to ensure proper contact on the arms.

SKILL 2   Forearm Pass

The following drills are designed to improve a player's forearm passing capability. These drills will begin by focusing on performing the movements correctly in a relatively stable environment. Task requirements and environment will then become more varied and difficult. The forearm pass drills will build from the concepts already introduced and practiced in the ready position and footwork sections.

I Toss–You Pass Drill

Have player stand on end line facing net with partner approximately 5 to 10 feet directly in front with back to net (see Figure 3.5). The player with his or her back to net is tosser while player on end line is passer. The tosser should toss high, easy balls for the passer to easily return to the tosser. The passer should not have to take more than one step to contact ball. Exchange positions after allotted time or hits.

Focus on . . .

1. Place ball correctly on forearms.
2. Keep hands together and arms straight.
3. Keep eyes focused on ball.

OPTIONS:

To decrease difficulty . . .   *Focus on . . .*

1. Have hitter let ball bounce once before contacting.   Lift from hips and legs.

2. Have hitter eliminate hit and simply try to catch or make contact on forearms.   Place ball correctly on forearms.

To increase difficulty . . .   *Focus on . . .*

1. Adjust the distance the tosser is from the hitter.   Hold hands and arms more parallel to ground as distance to tosser decreases; use legs more as distance increases.

2. Adjust tosses so that the hitter has to move forward, backward, or laterally to hit ball. Tell hitter where ball will be tossed at beginning.   Return to proper ready position. Get body under ball and in-line with target.

Checking for Skill Success: Touchdown Tester

The tosser will create a target for the hitter by raising his or her arms in the air after tossing the ball. The object is for the hitter to place the ball so that the tosser can catch the ball above the head and between the arms. If the hitter can do this without the tosser/catcher taking more than one step, he or she scores a touchdown and earns two points. If the tosser/catcher has to take more than one step or catches the ball below head level, he or she earns one point. After ten tosses, switch roles between the tosser and catcher.

▮ Continuous Partner Passing Drill

Partners face one another about 10 feet from each other (see Figure 3.6). One partner initiates toss to other, and partners keep ball in air as long as possible.

Focus on . . .
Start and maintain good ready position between hits.
Get body under ball and in-line with target.

OPTIONS:

To decrease difficulty . . .   *Focus on . . .*

1. Have hitters let ball bounce once before contacting.   Lift from hips and legs.

2. Catch and retoss after each hit.

To increase difficulty . . .   *Focus on . . .*

1. Have partners on opposite sides of net hitting back and forth.   Keep hands and arms together.

2. Limit hitting area to small 10-by-10-foot square.   Keep body in-line with target.

3. Have hitter contact ball once to self before hitting ball again to partner.   Get body under ball.

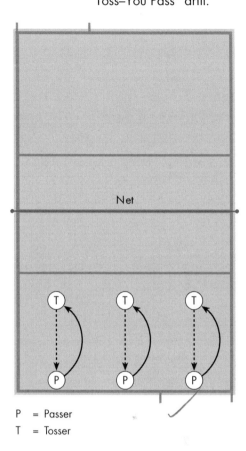

Figure 3.5
Positioning for "I Toss–You Pass" drill.

Net

P = Passer
T = Tosser

Figure 3.6 (on left)
"Continuous Partner Passing" drill.

Figure 3.7 (on right)
"Triangle Target Toss-and-Pass" drill.

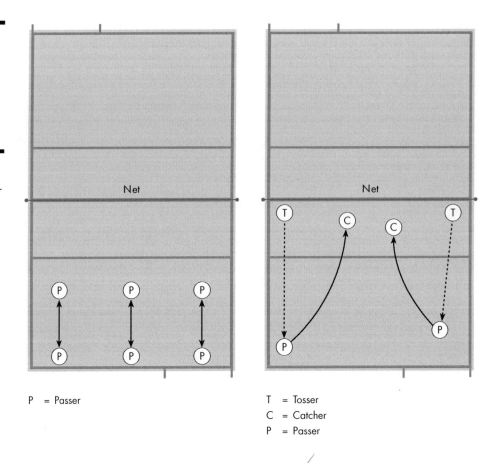

P = Passer

T = Tosser
C = Catcher
P = Passer

Triangle Target Toss-and-Pass Drill

In a group of three, have tosser toss ball to passer near end line (see Figure 3.7). The hitter should direct the ball to a catcher near the net and center of court.

Focus on . . .
Get body in-line with target (i.e., catcher).

OPTIONS:

To decrease difficulty . . .

1. Move all players closer together.
2. Have hitter try to simply direct ball to front of court.

Focus on . . .
Keep arms straight and together.

To increase difficulty . . .

1. Have tosser move to other side of net to initiate toss or serve.
2. Move location of catcher after every hit.
3. Move location of tosser so that incoming ball comes from various angles.
4. Have hitter run and touch attack line and shuffle backward to hitting area after the ball is contacted.

Focus on . . .
Use legs and not arms to generate force, if needed.

Have body in-line with target.

Return to good ready position between hits.

Keep eyes on incoming ball.

Continuous Triangle Partner Passing Drill

In a group of three, have partners form a triangle on the court (see Figure 3.8). One partner gently tosses ball in clockwise fashion to another partner, who passes to third partner. Continue to pass until an error is made. Restart toss again from person who made the error.

Focus on . . .

Get body under ball and in-line with target.

Keep eyes focused on ball.

OPTIONS:

To decrease difficulty . . .
1. Move players closer together.
2. Catch hitter's ball and toss to next partner.

Focus on . . .
Keep arms lower than shoulders throughout hit.

To increase difficulty . . .
1. Increase distance between partners.
2. Change direction of ball from clockwise to counterclockwise after it has been hit by all three players, or on command.
3. Increase number of players in group and/or number of pieces of equipment that are involved at one time. The more players that are involved, the more variety possible with the ball pathway.

Focus on . . .
Use hips and leg extension to generate power.

Get body under ball and in-line with target.

Figure 3.8

Continuous "Triangle Partner Passing" drill.

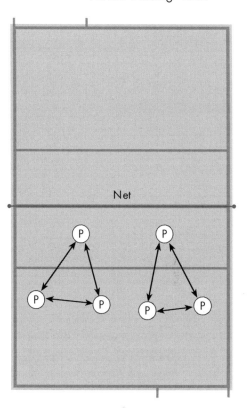

Net

P = Passer

Checking for Skill Success: Continuous Challenge

Each time your group can make the ball get around the triangle without an error, everyone scores a point. However, when an error is made, the group loses a point. The goal is to score ten points within a five-minute period.

Forearm Pass Modified Games

Hot Volley Tamales

Mexican music is played as partners are hitting ball around triangle. Whoever hits ball last when music stops is the "volley tamale." Each time a player becomes the volley tamale, he or she receives a letter to spell a word like *volley* or *tamale*.

Six vs. Six Toss/Hit/Grab Game ✓

Twelve or more players divide into two teams of six or more players each team. Players align themselves so that one team is on one side of the net while the other team is on the other. Three players on each team assume the role of front-row players while three are back-row players. Four balls are equally divided between the two teams. On the "go" command, teams toss the balls deep (past attack line) to their opponents' side of the court. The object of the back-row players is to forearm pass any incoming balls to the front-row players, who are the catchers. Every ball that is caught between the attack line and the net scores one point for that team. All tosses must be courtesy (i.e., easy). After an allotted amount of time or points, the game is stopped.

An option for lower-skilled students might include allowing more than one hit before the ball is caught. An option for more advanced players might include forcing them to touch a sideline or end line immediately after contacting the ball before resuming play. Thus, they have to hustle to get back into play.

Three vs. Three Half-Court Forearm Passing Game

Six players divide into two teams of three players each team. Players align themselves on half of a regulation court in a triangle formation and play a game of volleyball. The initial "serve" is from a toss. Rules can and should be adjusted depending on the skill level of the group and how well they have accomplished the previous drills. Some options might include allowing the ball to contact the floor between hits and allowing more than three hits to a side for less advanced players. Some options for more advanced players might include forcing them to have three contacts prior to the ball going over the net or having a hitter touch a sideline or end line immediately after contacting the ball before resuming play. Very advanced players can be allowed to play on a full court. The key to any rule change is to allow players of any ability to be successfully engaged in the game.

OVERHEAD PASS/SET

set or overhead pass
used to contact any
ball that is higher than
shoulder level with the
fingers and hands in an
overhead manner

Preview

The overhead pass or "set" is one of the most important skills in volleyball as it offers a player the most accuracy. The **set** is used to contact any ball that is higher than shoulder level with the fingers and hands in an overhand manner. Generally, the overhead pass is the second contact made after the serve, and its purpose is to set the ball to another teammate, who will spike it. Although the overhead pass or set can be performed after jumping or in a backward direction, these variations are more advanced techniques that will be briefly covered later in this section. Table 3.6 provides a short summary of the use of the overhead pass and its necessity in becoming a successful volleyball player. Table 3.7 provides a summary of the form characteristics or "cues" important for the proper execution of the overhead pass or set. This table also provides possible errors and causes of these errors. Figure 3.9 provides a visual representation of a properly performed overhead pass or set.

To overhead pass or set accurately and consistently, players must learn to get into proper position under the ball early. A "window" or triangle is formed with the thumbs and index fingers and the elbows are bent prior to contact with the ball.

TABLE 3.6	Overhead pass/set.	
SKILL	**USES**	**IMPORTANCE**
Overhead Passing/Setting	Contact balls that are higher than shoulder level.	Is extremely accurate if performed correctly. Allows more chances for creating attack situations.

TABLE 3.7	Overhead pass/set: Cues, errors, and causes.		
SKILL	**CUES**	**COMMON ERRORS**	**CAUSES OF ERRORS**
Overhead Pass/Set	▪ Body moves to get under ball and in-line with target.	Player mistimes the movement.	Eyes are not focused on the ball.
			Player is not getting under ball because of poor footwork or ready position.
	▪ Hands are open with fingers spread.		
	▪ Ball is contacted at head level.	Ball does not travel far.	Arms were already extended at contact.
	▪ Arms and legs extend towards target.	Ball travels directly upward or behind player after contact.	Ball is contacted directly above head instead of in front of forehead.
	▪ Eyes stay focused on ball.	Ball travels downward in direction.	Hands are closed and/ or used to slap at ball.

The hands are raised in front of the forehead and the ball is watched through the window of the hands. Since a slight lifting motion is needed by the legs as the ball is contacted, the knees must be bent and the back straight prior to contacting the ball. The shoulders are positioned squarely toward the target, and as the fingers contact the ball, the arms, hands, and legs extend toward the target.

Figure 3.9
A properly performed overhead pass.

a Ready   b Performance   c Follow-through

SKILL 3 | Overhead Pass/Set

The following drills are designed to improve players' overhead passing/setting capability. These drills will begin by focusing on performing the movement correctly in a relatively stable environment. The task requirements and environment will then become more varied and difficult. The overhead pass/set drills will build from the concepts already introduced and practiced in the preliminary and forearm pass sections.

▌I Toss–You Set Drill

Have player stand on end line facing net with partner approximately 5 to 10 feet directly in front with back to net (see Figure 3.10). The player with his or her back to net is tosser while player on end line is setter. The tosser should toss high, easy balls for the setter to easily return to the tosser. The setter should not have to take more than one step to contact ball. Exchange positions after allotted time or hits.

Focus on . . .

1. Place ball correctly on forearms.
2. Keep hands together and arms straight.
3. Keep eyes focused on ball.

OPTIONS:

To decrease difficulty . . .	*Focus on . . .*
1. Eliminate tosser and have setter set to self or after letting ball bounce off ground first.	Keep hands open with fingers spread. Contact ball at head level.
2. Have setter let ball bounce once before contacting.	Keep hands open with fingers spread. Contact ball at head level.
3. Have hitter eliminate hit and simply try to catch or make contact on forearms.	Contact ball at head level.

To increase difficulty . . .	*Focus on . . .*
1. Adjust the distance from the tosser to the setter.	Extend arms and legs toward target.
2. Adjust tosses so that the setter has to move forward, backward, or laterally to hit ball. Tell setter where ball will be tossed.	Return to proper ready position after each contact.
3. Perform continuous sets between partners.	Get body under ball and in-line with target.
4. Perform alternating forearm passes and sets.	Move body to get under ball and in-line with target.

Checking for Skill Success: Touchdown Tester

The tosser will create a target for the hitter by raising his or her arms in the air after tossing the ball. The object is for the hitter to place the ball so that the tosser can catch the ball above the head and between the arms. If the hitter can do this without the

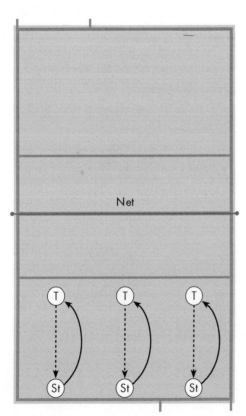

Figure 3.10
"I Toss–You Set" drill.

T = Tosser
St = Setter

tosser/catcher taking more than one step, he or she scores a touchdown and earns 2 points. If the tosser/catcher has to take more than one step or catches the ball below head level, he or she earns one point. After ten tosses, switch roles between the tosser and catcher.

Toss/Bump/Set Drill

In a group of three, have partners form a triangle on the court with two partners at the net and one near the end line (see Figure 3.11). The partner nearest the net pole gently tosses the ball to the passer who bumps the ball to the setter located at the midpoint of the court. The setter sets the ball back to the tosser/catcher. The passer should hit high, easy balls for the setter to easily return to the tosser. Setter should not have to take more than two steps to contact ball. If the pass to the setter is poor, have the bumper simply toss to the setter. Exchange positions after allotted time or hits.

Focus on . . .

1. Move body to get under ball and in-line with target.
2. Contact ball at head level.
3. Extend arms and legs toward target.
4. Keep eyes focused on ball.

OPTIONS:

To decrease difficulty . . .	Focus on . . .
1. Have setter let ball bounce once before contacting.	Move body to get under ball.
2. Have setter eliminate hit and simply try to catch ball.	Keep hands open with fingers spread. Contact ball at head level.

To increase difficulty . . .	Focus on . . .
1. Adjust hits and/or tosses so that the setter has to move to hit ball.	Return proper ready position. Get body under ball and in-line with target.
2. Add fourth player at other net pole area on court and take turns setting ball to original tosser/catcher or to newly added player on command or at random.	Get body under ball and in-line with target.

Checking for Skill Success: Hula Hoop Bowl Tester

In a group of three, have partners form a triangle on the court with two partners at the net and one near the end line. The partner nearest the net pole stands on a chair and holds a hula hoop parallel to the floor and level with the top of the net. The partner at the back of the court gently tosses the ball to the setter who attempts to set the ball up and through the hula hoop at the net. The tosser should toss high, easy balls for the setter to easily return to the hula hoop area. If the setter can place the ball directly through the hula hoop, he or she scores two points. If the ball hits the hoop or the holder the setter earns one point. After ten tosses, switch roles between the tosser, holder, and setter.

Figure 3.11
"Toss/Bump/Set"drill.

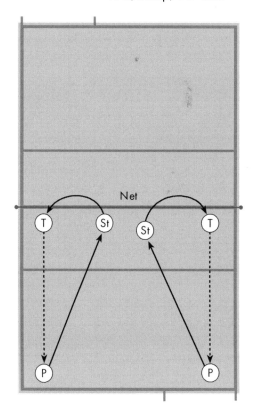

T = Tosser
P = Passer
St = Setter

Overhead Pass/Set Modified Games

Setting Basketball

Form two opposing teams of two to six players per team. The object of each team is to set the ball against a basketball backboard and make a basket. Each player on each opposing team gets to successively hit the ball after it has contacted the backboard and bounces on the floor once. Thus, after a player from team A gets a chance to set the ball and it bounces once on the floor, a player from team B gets a chance to set the ball. This rotation continues until the ball goes through the basket. If the ball bounces twice or is not playable (i.e., hit over backboard), the team who did not touch the ball last gets to resume play.

Three vs. Three Half-Court Forearm/Overhead Passing Game

Six players divide into two teams of three players per team. Players align themselves on half of a regulation court in a triangle formation and play a game of volleyball. The initial "serve" is from a toss. The emphasis in this game is the set. Thus, it can be played so that the second and third hits have to be overhead passes/sets, or at least one of the three hits on a side has to be a set. Rules can and should be adjusted depending on the skill level of the group and how well they have accomplished the previous drills. Some options might include allowing the ball to contact the floor between hits and allowing more than three hits to a side for less advanced players. Some options for more advanced players might include having a passer touch a side or end line immediately after contacting the ball before resuming play, and playing on a full court. The key to any rule change is to allow players of any ability to be successfully engaged in the game.

SERVE

Preview

serve *skill that puts the ball into play and is the only time that your team can earn points in an official game*

The **serve** is one of the most important skills in volleyball as it puts the ball in play and is the only time that your team can earn points in an official game. The serve is also different from other skills in volleyball as it is the only skill that is not influenced by other skills or the environment. In other words, the player has complete control in performing the skill. There are many different types of serves used in volleyball. The key to serving is placement and/or power. This section will only focus on the most fundamental serves (underhand and overhand floater). Table 3.8 provides a short summary of the use of the serve and its necessity in becoming a successful volleyball player. Table 3.9 provides a summary of the form characteristics or "cues" important for the proper execution of the serves. This table also provides possible errors and causes of these errors. Figures 3.12 and 3.13 provide visual representations of properly performed underhand and overhand floater serves.

To underhand serve accurately and consistently, players must learn to hold the ball out in front of the body with one hand and hit it from below with the other. The ball can be effectively struck with the hand, fist or wrist; with the heel of the hand providing an especially effective hitting surface. Additional power is generated by stepping forward with the foot opposite of the hitting hand while striking the ball. The hitting hand follows through toward the top of the net after contact.

The overhand floater serve is performed by tossing the ball upward and in front of the serving arm. The toss should be made with little or no spin on the ball. The feet are staggered with the foot opposite the hitting hand placed in front of the

TABLE 3.8	Serve.	
SKILL	**USES**	**IMPORTANCE**
Underhand Serve	To easily get ball into play.	Allows for maximum accuracy if performed correctly.
		Allows for greater success on part of beginner player.
Overhand Floater Serve	To get ball into play with greater speed and provide greater variability for opponents.	Speed and unpredictable flight of ball make it difficult to return.

TABLE 3.9	Serve: Cues, errors, and causes.		
SKILL	**CUES**	**COMMON ERRORS**	**CAUSES OF ERRORS**
Underhand Serve	■ Ball is hit at waist level out of opposite hand.	Ball travels directly upward or behind player after contact.	Ball is contacted too high and not at waist level.
	■ Nondominant foot is forward.	Ball travels in direction other than what was intended.	Body is not facing target.
	■ Heel of open hand is used to contact ball.		Follow-through of hand is not toward top of net.
	■ Weight shifts to front foot at contact.	Ball does not travel very far.	Holding hand is moving
	■ Follow-through of hand is toward top of net.		No step is taken during contact.
Overhand Floater Serve	■ Ball is tossed with one hand in front of body.	Ball travels directly upward or is hit past opponent's end line.	Ball is contacted over head instead of in front of body.
	■ Nondominant foot is forward.		Player tries to hit ball too hard.
	■ Ball is contacted by heel of open hand with arm fully extended.	Ball travels in direction other than what was intended.	Body is not facing target.
			Toss is inconsistent.
	■ Weight shifts to front foot at contact.	Ball does not travel over net.	No step is taken during contact.
	■ Hand does not follow through after contact.		Ball is contacted too far away from hitting arm.

other foot. The body is turned in the direction the ball is to travel. The body weight is transferred from the rear foot to the front foot, as in the underhand serve, by stepping forward while striking the ball. The ball is struck with the heel of the hitting hand with the arm fully extended above the head. There is no follow-through of the hand after the hit.

Figure 3.12
A properly performed
underhand floater serve.

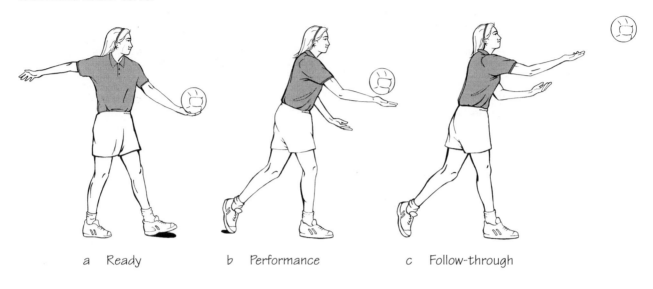

a   Ready   b   Performance   c   Follow-through

Figure 3.13
A properly performed
overhand floater serve.

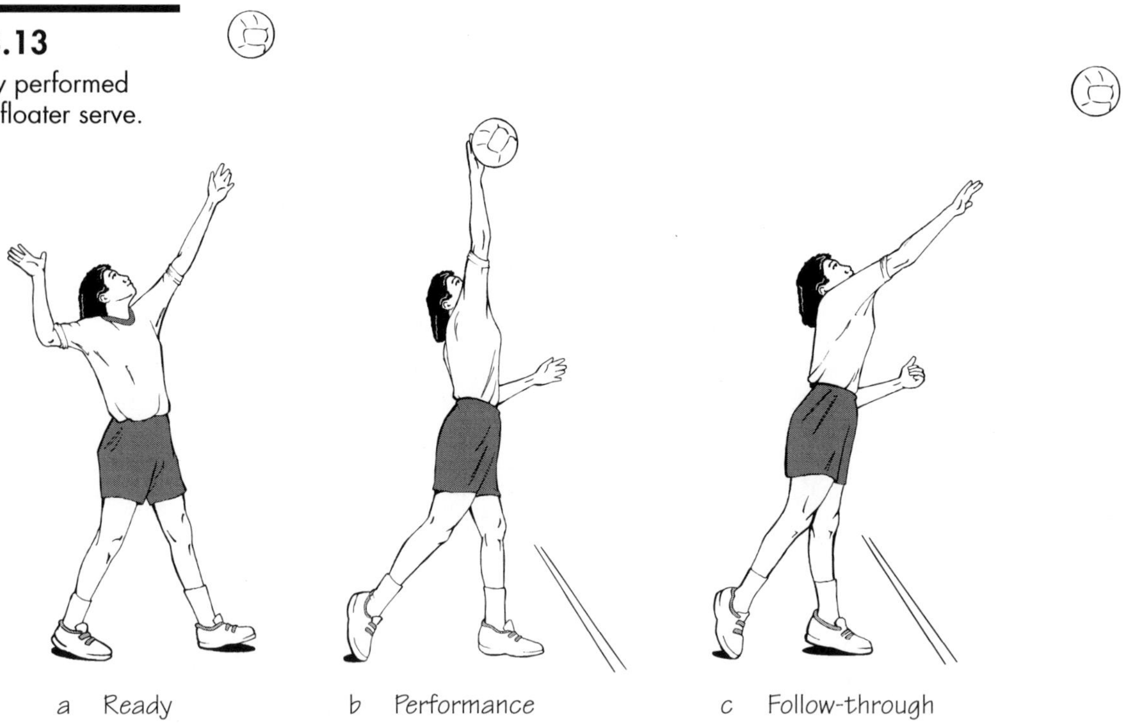

a   Ready   b   Performance   c   Follow-through

SKILL 4 Serve

The following drills are designed to improve players' serving capability. These
drills will begin by focusing on performing the movement correctly in a relatively
stable environment. The drills will then become more difficult as other skills are
added. The serve drills build from the concepts already introduced and practiced in
the preliminary, forearm pass, and overhead pass/set sections.

I Serve–You Fetch Drill

Partners stand in opposite sides of the court, starting 10 to 15 feet from the net (see Figure 3.14). One partner will serve the ball over the net while the other partner retrieves. The partner who retrieves the ball will serve back over the net.

Focus on . . .

1. Shift weight.
2. Strike ball at appropriate contact point.
3. Follow through after underhand serve.

OPTIONS:

To decrease difficulty . . .

1. Have partners start closer together.
2. Have servers perform movement without contacting ball.
3. Lower or take away net.

Focus on . . .
Use heel of open hand to contact ball.

To increase difficulty . . .

1. Have server use nondominant hand.
2. Have server serve to specified locations (use tape or cones, or simply move partner after each hit) of court. Encourage end line and sideline placement.

Focus on . . .
Step with dominant foot during contact with ball.
Face body toward target area
Follow through in direction of intended ball landing location for underhand serve.

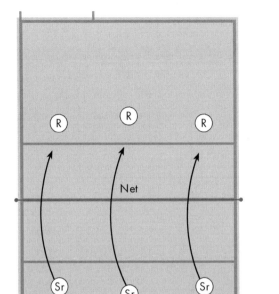

Figure 3.14
"I Serve–You Fetch" drill.

R = Retriever
Sr = Server

Checking for Skill Success: Serve Spot Test

Each side of the volleyball court is divided into nine equal squared areas: three by the end line, three in the middle of the court, and three along the net. Each area is numbered. All players have partners. One player is the server. The partner, a caller/recorder, selects an area for the server to serve to prior to initiating the serve. If the server can direct the ball into the correct area as called by the partner, the server receives three points. If the ball lands in one of the adjoining areas from the intended one, the server receives two points. If the ball lands in fair territory but not in an adjoining area, the server receives one point. After ten serves, switch roles between the server and the caller/recorder.

Serve/Bump/Catch Drill

In a group of three, one partner is the server. The other two partners are located on the other side of the net. One player is near end line while other player is nearer to net (see Figure 3.15). The object is for the server to direct the ball to the player near the end line. This player is to forearm pass ball to player near the net. The player at the net is to catch ball. The passer should not have to take more than three steps to contact ball. If two serves to the passer are poor, the catcher should simply toss a ball to the passer who forearm passes it back to catcher. Exchange positions after allotted time or hits.

Focus on . . .

1. Square body to target during serve.

2. Be in good ready position prior to forearm pass.
3. Use follow-through for underhand serves.
4. When serving, step with nondominant foot during contact with ball.

OPTIONS:

To decrease difficulty . . .

1. Have forearm passer or server move closer to net.
2. Have more than one forearm passer in backcourt to increase target area.

Focus on . . .

Use heel of open hand to contact ball during serve.

To increase difficulty . . .

1. Have server serve from behind end line.

2. Move forearm passer to new location after each serve.
3. Add another player at net so that one player is closer to center and other is closer to sideline. Player at the center of net should set forearm passes while player nearer to sideline catches the sets.

Focus on . . .

Step with nondominant foot during contact with ball.

Square body toward target.

Get under ball and face target before setting ball.

Serving Modified Games

Horseshoe Serverama

In a group of four, have players divide into two teams. As in regular horseshoes, have each set of partners stand on opposite sides of the court, starting 10 to 15 feet from the net (see Figure 3.16). Each set of partners has two balls. On the court

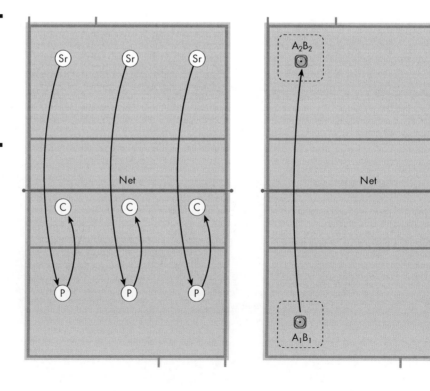

Figure 3.15 (on left)
"Serve/Bump/Catch" drill.

Sr = Server
P = Passer
C = Catcher

Figure 3.16 (on right)
Horseshoe Serverama.

Team A=A₁ and A₂
Team B=B₁ and B₂

floor, there arc two marked areas with a cone in the center. The object is to serve the ball over the net so that it lands in the marked area or hits the cone. Each set of players get two chances to score points. One point is scored for each ball that lands in the marked area whereas two points are scored for each ball that contacts a cone. Options include widening or narrowing the marked areas. In addition, the players can be moved closer or farther away from the net depending on skill level.

Three vs. Three Half-Court Serve/Bump/Set/Hit Game

Six players divide into two teams with three players on each team. Players align themselves on half of a regulation court in a triangle formation and play a game of volleyball. The ball is served from the back right area of the court. The emphasis of this game is the combination of all skills. Thus, it is not important whether the serving team rotates players after a side-out or after every serve. However, it is suggested that teams be required to use a pass-set-hit (i.e., pass, set, open-hand standing hit) sequence before the ball goes over the net. Rules can and should be adjusted depending on the skill level of the group and how well they have accomplished the previous drills. Some options also include allowing the ball to contact the floor between hits, making the court smaller, having the server start closer to the net, and allowing more than three hits to a side for less advanced players. Some options for more advanced players might include having a passer touch a side or end line immediately after contacting the ball before resuming play, and playing on a full court. The key to any rule change is to allow players of any ability to be successfully engaged in the game.

Preview

The **spike** is the most powerful skill in volleyball and involves the explosive action of hitting the ball hard and downward over the net into the opponent's court at a sharp angle. Besides being the most crowd-pleasing skill of the game, it is a team's most lethal weapon for ending a rally. Unfortunately, the spike is also one of the most difficult skills to learn. In order to make a successful spike, a player must jump in the air and hit a small moving object, the ball, over an obstacle, the net, so that it lands in a small area, the court. Due to the many variables associated with spiking, timing and execution are difficult at best. Table 3.10 provides a short summary of the use of the spike and its necessity in becoming a successful volleyball player. Table 3.11 provides a summary of the form characteristics or "cues" important for the proper execution of the spike. This table also provides possible errors and causes of these errors. Figure 3.17 provides a visual representation of a properly performed spike.

To spike accurately and consistently, players must learn to convert their forward momentum toward the net into vertical jumping height. To do this, players need to approach the ball by covering as much area as possible with as few steps as possible. The spiker will take a long last step by jumping forward, contacting the floor first with the heel of one foot and then with the heel of the other foot with the

SPIKE

spike skill that involves hitting the ball hard and downward over the net into the opponent's court at a sharp angle

TABLE 3.10 Spiking.		
SKILL	**USES**	**IMPORTANCE**
Spike	To quickly score point, earn side-out, and exert control over an opponent.	The ball travels very quickly, thus shortening the time defensive players have to react to the flight of the ball.

Figure 3.17
A properly performed spike.

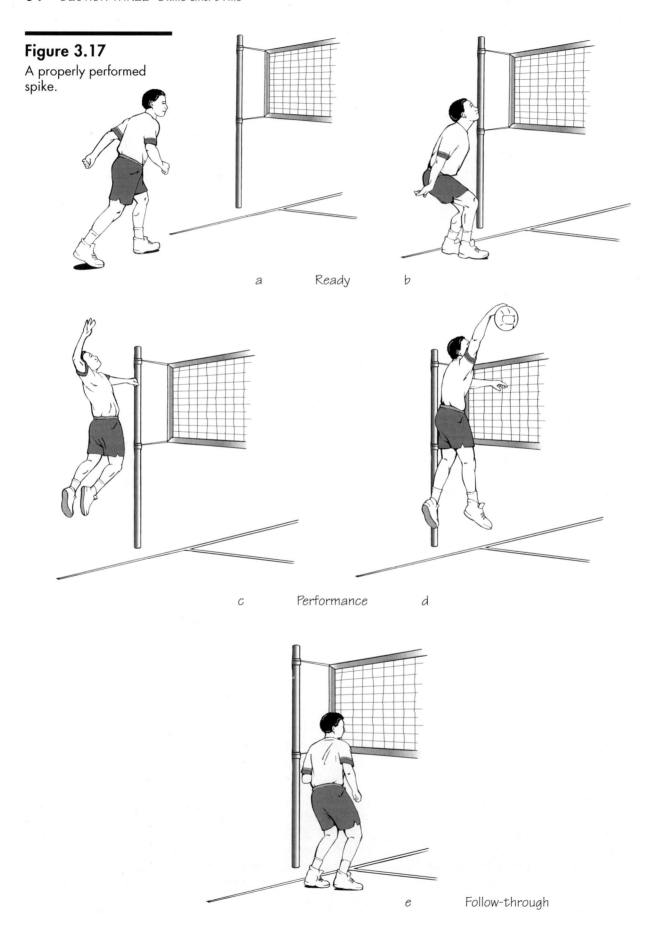

a   Ready   b

c   Performance   d

e   Follow-through

TABLE 3.11 Spiking: Cues, errors, and causes.

SKILL	CUES	COMMON ERRORS	CAUSES OF ERRORS
Spike	■ Last two steps are step/close and jump. ■ Jump is vertical. ■ Open hand contacts ball. ■ Ball is contacted in front of hitting shoulder with arm fully extended. ■ Player lands on both feet.	Spiker has to stop and wait for set. Net is touched by body. Ball is hit out of bounds. Ball is hit into net.	Ball is too far away prior to starting approach. Set is too close to net or player is not planting both feet prior to jumping so that jump is vertical. Ball is contacted beneath its midline. Ball is too far from body before contact.

weight rolling from both heels to the toes as the player takes off. The arms swing high as the player jumps straight into the air. The hitting arm is drawn back with the elbow high and hand close to the ear. The hitting arm swings to hit the ball in front of the hitting shoulder. The player lands on both feet.

SKILL 5 Spike

The following drills are designed to improve players' spiking capability. These drills will begin by focusing on performing the movement correctly in a relatively stable environment and will progressively become more difficult as other skills are added. The spike drills build from the concepts already introduced and practiced in the preliminary, forearm pass, setting, and serving sections.

I Hold–You Hit Drill

Players are in groups of three. One player holds a ball above the net while standing on a chair. Another player is waiting at the attack line to hit the held ball while a third player is on the other side of the net waiting to retrieve hit balls (see Figure 3.18). The hitter practices a simple approach and hits the ball out of the partner's hand and over the net.

Focus on . . .
1. Start in ready position.
2. Step/close and jump.
3. Hit with open hand.

OPTIONS:

To decrease difficulty . . .
1. Have spiker hit without a net.
2. Instruct spiker to jump and hit from stationary position.
3. Have spiker carry ball while approaching net and jump and throw ball down over net, snapping wrist.

Focus on . . .
Hit downward.
Contact ball with open hand.
Contact ball in front of hitting shoulder with arm fully extended.

Figure 3.18 (on left)
"I Hold–You Hit" drill.

Figure 3.19 (on right)
"I Throw–You Go" drill.

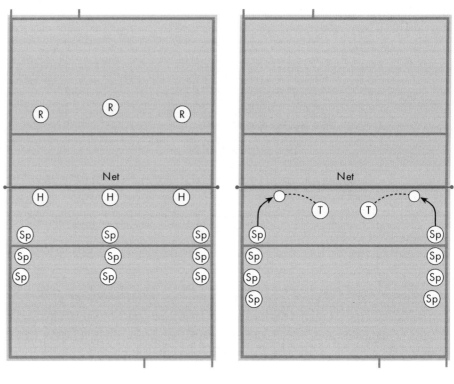

H = Holder   T = Tosser
Sp = Spiker   Sp = Spiker
R = Retriever

To increase difficulty . . .   *Focus on . . .*
1. Have spiker use nondominant hand.   Jump vertically.
2. Hold ball at various heights and   Land on both feet.
   locations about net.
3. Have ball tossed instead of held.

I Throw–You Go Drill

Players are arranged in two groups with a tosser at the net and spikers in a hitting line (see Figure 3.19). The tosser tells the spiker "ready." This signals the player who is waiting at attack line to be ready to react to and spike ball. The tosser directs the ball high above and a few feet from the net. The hitter practices a simple approach and spike over the net. The spiker retrieves his or her own ball.

Focus on . . .
1. Start in ready position.
2. Step/close and jump.
3. Jump vertically.

OPTIONS:

To decrease difficulty . . .   *Focus on . . .*
1. Have spiker start closer to net.   Step/close and jump.
2. Lower net.

To increase difficulty . . .

1. Instruct spiker to use nondominant hand.
2. Vary tosses so that ball path or trajectory is different each throw.
3. Have ball tossed from nondominant or off-hand side of body.

Focus on . . .

Contact ball with open hand.

Contact ball in front of hitting shoulder with arm fully extended. Land on both feet.

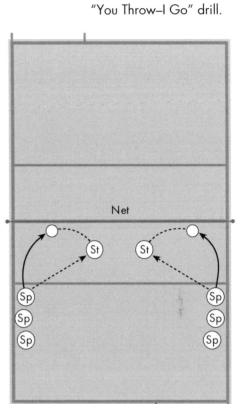

Figure 3.20
"You Throw–I Go" drill.

St = Setter
Sp = Spiker

You Throw–I Go Drill

Players are in groups so that there is a setter and a spiking line (see Figure 3.20). The setter tells the spiker "ready." This signals the spiker who is waiting at attack line to be ready to toss ball to setter. After the ball is tossed from the would-be spiker, the setter directs the ball high above and a few feet from the net. The spiker reacts to the set ball and practices a simple approach and spike over the net.

Focus on . . .

1. Contact ball with open hand.
2. Step/close and jump.
3. Jump vertically.

OPTIONS:

To decrease difficulty . . .

1. Have spiker start closer to net.
2. Lower net.
3. Have setter simply toss to spiker.

Focus on . . .
Step/close and jump.

To increase difficulty . . .

1. Instruct spiker to use nondominant hand.
2. Vary toss so that ball path or trajectory is different each throw.
3. Vary distance of setter from spiker.

4. Have ball set from nondominant or off-hand side of body.
5. Encourage spiking for accuracy of location by using targets.

Focus on . . .

Contact ball with open hand.

Contact ball in front of hitting shoulder with arm fully extended. Land on both feet.

As distance from setter diminishes, decrease angle of approach to spike.

Contact ball at full arm extension.

Checking for Skill Success: You Go–I Check Test

Use previous drill to detect whether players are successfully spiking a tossed/set ball. Have each player spike at least ten balls on both dominant side (i.e., on-hand side) and nondominant side of the body.

Figure 3.21

"Serve/Pass/Set/Spike" drill.

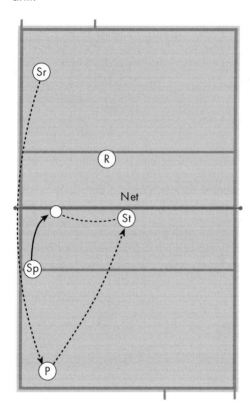

P = Passer
Sp = Spiker
R = Retriever
St = Setter
Sr = Server

Serve/Pass/Set/Spike Drill

In a group of five, one player is a server. Another player is a passer near the end line, while a third player is a setter at the net. A fourth player is at the attack line ready to spike. The fifth player is on the same side of the net as the server and acts as a ball retriever (see Figure 3.21). The object is for the server to direct the ball to the player near the end line. This player is to forearm pass ball to player near the net, who sets to the spiker. The spiker should spike ball over net to the retriever, who hands ball back to server. Players should not have to take more than three steps to contact ball. If a ball has been hit poorly, the ball should be tossed to player who errored. If player errors again, the ball can be self-tossed. Exchange positions after allotted time or hits.

Focus on . . .
1. Start in ready position.
2. Keep head up and body focused in direction of movement.
3. Move to get under ball.

OPTIONS:

To decrease difficulty . . .
1. Have forearm passer or server move closer to net.
2. Have balls tossed instead of hit.

Focus on . . .
Use heel of open hand to contact ball.

To increase difficulty . . .
1. Have server serve from behind end line.
2. Move forearm passer to new location after each serve.
3. Add a sixth player at net near opposite sideline so that setter is in center and other two are at opposites sidelines ready to spike. Player at the center of net should receive forearm passes and alternate sets between spikers.

Focus on . . .
Step with nondominant foot during contact with ball.
When serving, square body to target.
When setting, get under ball and face target before contact.

Spiking Modified Games

King/Queen of the Court

Players form teams of three and line up behind an end line. One team of three is selected to line up on the other side (king/queen side) of the net. The first team of three moves onto the vacant half of the court and serves the ball to the king/queen side. The ball is rallied until play is over (the ball is hit out or the ball is not returned over the net). If the king/queen team wins the rally, that team scores a point and remains on its side of the court. If the challenger side wins the rally, that team replaces the team on the king/queen side. The players on the losing team return to the end of the line. Points can only be scored when on the king/queen side. Play should be somewhat continuous as the next team may serve immediately after a point or king/queen change has been made. Since the spike is the emphasis of this game, the king/queen side can be required to complete a three-hit (bump-set-spike) attack sequence after the serve. After this sequence, any number of hits might be used prior to hitting the ball over the net.

Three vs. Three Half-Court Serve/Bump/Set/Spike Game

Six players divide into two teams of three players per team. Players align themselves on half of a regulation court in a triangle formation and play a game of volleyball. The ball is served from the back right area of the court. The emphasis of this game is the combination of skills. Thus, it is not important whether the serving team rotates players after a side-out or after every serve. However, it is suggested that teams be required to use a pass-set-spike sequence before the ball goes over the net. Rules can and should be adjusted depending on the skill level of the group and how well they have accomplished the previous drills. Some options might include allowing the ball to contact the floor between hits, making the court smaller, having the server start closer to the net, and allowing more than three hits to a side for less advanced players. Some options for more advanced players might include having a passer touch a side or end line immediately after contacting the ball before resuming play, and playing on a full court. The key to any rule change is to allow players of any ability to be successfully engaged in the game.

BLOCK

Preview

The **block** is a defensive play by one or more players who attempt to intercept the ball near the net. The block creates a physical barrier for the spiker to try to hit around. The greater the obstacle (i.e., multiple blockers), the harder it is to spike as there is less court area to hit into. Since players can reach over the net during a block, the block has become an effective weapon as well as a defense. The only stipulation in reaching over the net is that the ball cannot be touched until the opposing team has completed its attack. Table 3.12 provides a short summary of the use of the block and its necessity in becoming a successful volleyball player. Table 3.13 provides a summary of the form characteristics or "cues" important for the proper execution of the block. This table also provides possible errors and causes of these errors. Figure 3.22 provides a visual representation of a properly performed single block, whereas Figure 3.23 illustrates a multiple block.

> **block** defensive skill that involves intercepting the ball from an opponent's contact near the net

To block accurately and consistently, players must learn to watch the setter and the intended spiker. From the ready position, the blocker needs to adjust so that he or she is lined up one-half body width toward the spiker/hitter's hitting side. The blocker's shoulders remain parallel to the net. Once the body is positioned, the blocker will jump immediately after the spiker/hitter jumps. The fingers and hands are spread to cover as much area as possible with the arms going over the net to stop the approaching ball. The elbows are locked with the hands positioned to both sides of the hitter's hitting arm. The blocker should land on both feet on his or her side of the court.

TABLE 3.12	Blocking.	
SKILL	**USES**	**IMPORTANCE**
Block	To prevent ball from entering your side of court.	Intimidates spikers. Forces other team to keep ball on its side of court. Forces other team to make errors.

TABLE 3.13 Blocking: Cues, errors, and causes.

SKILL	CUES	COMMON ERRORS	CAUSES OF ERRORS
Single Block	■ Lined up one-half body width toward the spiker's hitting side. ■ Shoulders remain parallel to the net. ■ Jump is vertical and from ready position. ■ Fingers and hands are spread. ■ Hands are positioned to both sides of the hitter's hitting arm. ■ Player lands on both feet.	Ball is not contacted. Spiker hits around blocker's hands. Ball contacts hands but lands on blocker's side of net. Net is touched by body.	Jumped too soon or too late. Fingers of hands are closed. Body is out of position from spiker. Shoulders are not square to net. Jump is not vertical. Hands are not retracted after block.
Multiple Block	■ Primary blocker gets in position first. ■ Assisting blocker is responsible for getting in position next to primary blocker. ■ Assisting blocker is responsible for spike hit at an angle crosscourt.	Blockers run into one another. Spiker hits around both blocker's hands.	Joining blocker is not positioning with the primary blocker. Joining blocker is watching spiker and not primary blocker. Joining blocker is trying to block ball instead of angle from the primary blocker.

Figure 3.22

A properly performed single block.

a Ready   b Performance   c Follow-through

Figure 3.23
A properly performed multiple block.

a   Ready

b   Performance

The execution of a multiple block is performed similarly to the single block. The main difference is how players position themselves to create the largest obstacle for the spiker/hitter. When the block is on the outside of the court, the outside player sets the block and the middle player positions himself or herself with the outside player. When the block will be made in the middle of the court, one or both outside players will position themselves alongside the middle blocker. The key is to watch the primary blocker's alignment and then to adjust one's own position next to the primary blocker's.

SKILL | 6 | Blocking

Let's Get Touchy-Feely

Players will partner-up on opposite sides of the net (see Figure 3.24). Each partner is about 2 feet from the net. On command, students will jump and touch each other's hands above net as in giving each other a high five.

Focus on . . .
Jump from ready position.
Jump vertically with fingers and hands spread.

c   Follow-through

Figure 3.24
"Let's Get Touchy-Feely" drill.

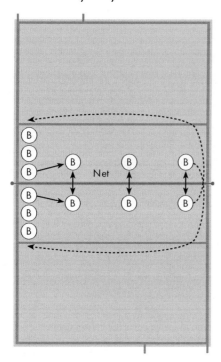

B = Blocker

Figure 3.25
"Attackers vs. Blockers" drill.

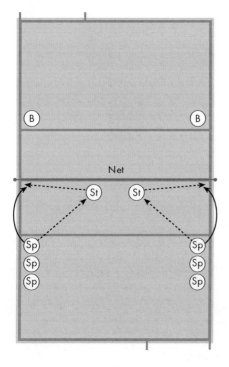

Sp = Spiker   St = Setter   B = Blocker

OPTIONS:

To decrease difficulty . . .

1. Use wall instead of partner or net.

Focus on . . .

Jump as high as possible vertically.

To increase difficulty . . .

1. Have players reach hands and arms in different directions: block right, left, and straight up.

2. Have players move down the net touching partners' hands as they go.

3. Position partners with one at net and other at attack line with ball. Player with ball tosses slightly above net. The blocker attempts to block ball back. Balls may be tossed to right or left as skill increases.

4. Have several players standing on chairs on one side of net at the left, center, and right front positions. These players reach a ball slightly over the top of the net. Other players move down the net and take the ball with two hands to their side of the net. They give ball back and slide to next position along net to block.

Focus on . . .

Have hands and fingers spread.

Keep shoulders parallel to the net.

Position hands to both sides of the hitter's hitting arm.

Keep shoulders parallel to the net.

▌Attackers vs. Blockers

Players form four lines with two at each sideline near the net (see Figure 3.25). The spiking line tosses a ball to a setter, who sets back to the spiker, who attempts a spike. The blocker in the blocking line attempts to stop the spike. After each player has performed a skill, he or she travels to the other side of the net near the opposite sideline to practice the other skill.

Focus on . . .

Concentrate on the spiker, not only on the ball.

OPTIONS:

To decrease difficulty . . .

1. Have setter toss balls to spikers.
2. Have spiker hold ball instead of hit.

Focus on . . .

Keep shoulders square to net.

To increase difficulty . . .

1. Include double block with assisting blocker starting nearer to setter.

2. Have tosser vary location of tosses for spiker.

Focus on . . .

Move in position with primary blocker.

Keep eyes focused on spiker.

Checking for Skill Success: Attackers vs. Blockers Test

Same drill as before. Players or recorder keeps track of successful blocks. A block that at least contacts the ball, whether or not it was successful, scores a point. A block that forces the ball back into the opponents' side of the court scores two points. Each player should have ten opportunities to block.

Serve Pass/Set/Spike/Block Drill

In a group of five or six, one player is a server. Another player is a passer near the end line, while a third player is at the net near the sideline as a setter. A fourth player is at the attack line ready to spike. The fifth and sixth players are on the same side of the net as the server and act as the blockers (see Figure 3.26). The object is for the server to direct the ball to the player near the end line. This player is to forearm pass ball to player near the net, who sets to the spiker. The spiker should spike the ball over net while the blocker attempts to stop it. Players should not have to take more than three steps to contact ball. If a ball has been hit poorly, the ball should be tossed to player who errored. If this player errors again, the ball can be self-tossed. Exchange positions after allotted time or hits.

Focus on . . .
1. Start in ready position.
2. Keep head up and body focused in direction of movement.
3. Move to get under ball.

OPTIONS:

To decrease difficulty . . .
1. Have forearm passer or server move closer to net.
2. Have balls tossed instead of hit.

Focus on . . .
Use heel of open hand to contact ball.

To increase difficulty . . .
1. Have server serve from behind end line.
2. Move forearm passer to new location after each serve.
3. Add a sixth player to initiate double block.

Focus on . . .
Step with nondominant foot during contact.
While serving, square body of server toward target.

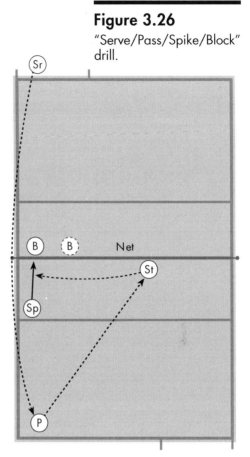

Figure 3.26
"Serve/Pass/Spike/Block" drill.

Sr = Server
St = Setter
B = Blocker
P = Passer
Sp = Spiker

Blocking Modified Games

Three vs. Three Serve/Bump/Set/Spike/Block Game

Six players divide into two teams of three players per team. Players align themselves on half of a regulation court in a triangle formation and play a game of volleyball. The ball is served from the back right area of the court. The emphasis of this game is the combination of all skills. It is suggested that teams be required to use a pass-set-spike sequence before the ball goes over the net. Rules can and should be adjusted depending on the skill level of the group and how well they have accomplished the previous drills. Since spiking and blocking are being emphasized, allowing more than three hits on a side might be an appropriate rule modification. Some other options might include allowing the ball to contact the floor between hits, making the court smaller, and having the server start closer to the net. Some options for more advanced players might include having a passer touch a side or end line immediately after contacting the ball and before resuming play, and playing on a full court. The key to any rule change is to allow players of any ability to be successfully engaged in the game.

ADVANCED SKILLS

Although we have discussed the basic skills used in volleyball, there are several advanced skills that need to be mentioned. Advanced skills are important as they help players advance to higher levels of competition and game success. Table 3.14 provides a short summary of the use of these skills and their importance in becom-

TABLE 3.14 Advanced skills.

SKILL	USES	IMPORTANCE
Dig	To prevent very low and hard-hit ball from touching floor.	Keeps in play a ball that has been spiked. Frustrates spikers.
Lateral Pass	To contact balls when there is not enough time to face target.	Keeps low balls in play.
One-Arm Pass	To contact low balls that are too far away to contact with two arms.	Keeps low balls in play.
Backward Pass	Used by backcourt players to recover and contact partially blocked balls when there is not enough time to face toward net or target.	Keeps blocked balls in play.
Back Set	Allows the set to be made to a spiker without having to face him or her.	Helps to deceive the opponent's blockers. Allows a spiker a greater chance of success as the location of a spike is not telegraphed to potential blockers by the setter.
Jump Set	Allows the setter to decrease the trajectory of the set ball to the spiker. Provides the setter the option of spiking or setting.	Allows team to speed up attack sequence. Helps to deceive the opponent's blockers into preparing for a spike.
Topspin Serve	Provides for abrupt downward trajectory of ball during service.	Makes ball hard to return as it travels fast and downward over the net.
Jump-Spike Serve	Provides for hard serve that is in air minimal time.	Makes ball hard to return as the amount of time to get under the ball is minimal.
Dink	Allows for the soft directing of the ball from a spiking approach to a vacant area on court.	Helps to deceive the opponents, who are prepared to defend a hard spike.

Figure 3.27 (on left)
A properly performed dig.

Figure 3.28 (on right)
A properly performed lateral pass.

ing a successful volleyball player. Although these skills are beyond the scope of this text, a brief explanation is provided that explains the proper execution of each advanced skill. Most of these advanced skills are simply modifications of basic skills already mentioned and can be utilized interchangeably in the drills presented in this section.

Dig

A dig is basically the same skill as the forearm pass except that it originates from a spiked ball instead of a served ball. Thus, the ball is traveling much faster and with greater force. This has several implications for the player trying to execute this skill. Since the ball is traveling so quickly, it is generally contacted low to the ground. The ball should not be hit, but allowed to simply rebound off the forearms. The wrists should be flexed to allow the ball to gain enough height to be set (see Figure 3.27).

Lateral Pass

A lateral pass is used when there is not enough time to position the body toward the intended target for a forearm pass attempt. A player has to dip his/her front shoulder forward with the interior part of the forearms toward the target. The weight of the player is mainly over the front leg. Although this is a rather difficult skill to accomplish, it can help players retrieve balls they might not otherwise get when they are caught out of position (see Figure 3.28).

One-Arm Pass

A one-arm pass is used when the ball is too far away to contact with a lateral pass. This desperation hit simply tries to keep the ball playable for a teammate. A player attempting a one-handed pass should contact the ball on the forearm if at all possible (see Figure 3.29).

Figure 3.29
A player attempting a one-arm pass.

Figure 3.30
A properly performed
backward pass.

Backward Pass

The backward pass is often used by a backcourt player to recover balls hit off the top of the blocker's hands or from an errant hit. The main goal of this forearm pass is to simply keep the ball in play or to hit it over the net. It is especially hard to place the ball since the passer is not looking toward where they are hitting the ball. The key to a successful backward pass is to lift the forearms above shoulder level and to lean back during the contact (see Figure 3.30).

Back Set

The back set is used to direct the ball to a spiker behind the setter. Thus, the back set can be effective in confusing the blockers. The back set utilizes the same initial body position as the front set. The only difference is that the hands of the setter contact the ball above the head with the arms extending and the back arching during the set. The wrists do not make their normal extension forward, but rather remain in the palm-up position. It is important that the ball be set upward and backward rather than just backward (see Figure 3.31).

Jump Set

The jump set is performed the same way as a regular set except that it is performed while in midair. The setter should take off either exactly underneath the ball or from such a distance that when contact is made, the body is underneath the ball. The setting action should take place at the peak of the jump. The jump set can be particularly effective as it can deceive an opposing blocker into thinking that the setter is spiking. This skill can also be effective in saving a pass or dig that is headed over the net (see Figure 3.32).

Figure 3.31 (on left)
A properly performed
back set.

Figure 3.32 (on right)
A properly performed
jump set.

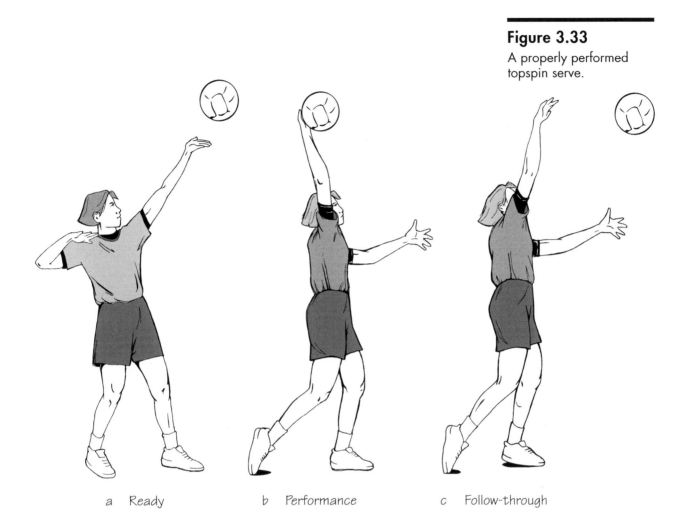

Figure 3.33
A properly performed
topspin serve.

a Ready b Performance c Follow-through

Topspin Serve

The topspin serve is very effective as it rises slightly after contact, but drops suddenly once it begins its descent. Because of its abrupt downward curve, it is not in the air long, cutting down the receiver's response time. The starting position for the topspin serve is similar to the starting position for the floater serve. However, the toss is higher, with the player bending deeply at the knees. The power needed to create the spin is generated from straightening the legs. The ball is contacted with an open, slightly cupped palm. The heel of the hand should contact the ball first and the fingers should come over the top, turning the ball forward with a topspin. The arm should be fully extended at contact (see Figure 3.33).

Jump-Spike Serve

The jump-spike serve is a powerful serve that flies through the air very quickly. This is an effective serve as the receiver's response time is very short. This is also a difficult serve as the server must toss the ball out in front of the body and run and jump to hit it high in the air. The key to this skill is to toss the ball inside the court area and take off before reaching the end line. The ball is hit in a spikelike movement toward the net. Obviously, the trajectory is much straighter than the topspin serve (see Figure 3.34).

Figure 3.34

A properly performed jump-spike serve.

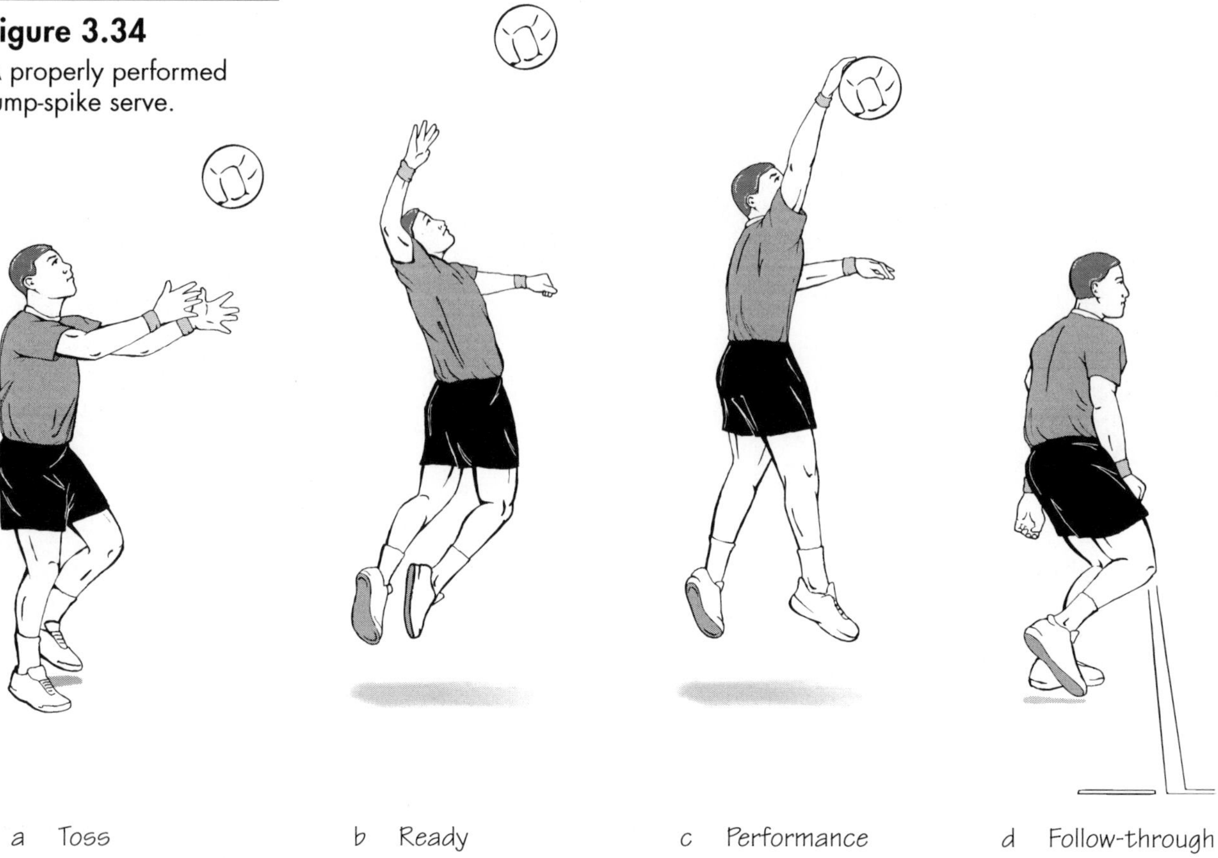

a   Toss   b   Ready   c   Performance   d   Follow-through

Figure 3.35

A properly performed dink.

Dink

The dink is basically a soft spike used to catch the defensive team off guard. It is especially effective from a good set when the opponent's team is expecting a hard-driven spike. The spiker should cock the spiking arm in the normal manner and swing at a much reduced speed to contact the ball with the fingertips. Contact of the ball should take place as high over the net as possible so that the ball can be tipped over the blockers. A low dink will usually result in the ball being stuffed by the blocker on the spiker/dinker's side of the net (see Figure 3.35).

Strategies

Strategy in volleyball is part physical and part psychological. The physical provides the mechanics to execute what the mental suggests needs to be done to win a point. Both are equally important to develop.

The role of the mind and its impact on sport performance is the cornerstone of an emerging field of study known as sport psychology. Today, coaches and athletes readily acknowledge the central role that psychological factors play in sport performance. The important point, however, is that the proper mental attitude or focus is necessary and beneficial at all levels of athletic participation, from the beginner through the professional, and the psychological skills needed to be successful can be learned by virtually anyone. The following sections will discuss four prominent psychological skills all athletes should strive to possess.

PSYCHOLOGICAL STRATEGIES FOR PERFORMANCE ENHANCEMENT

Mental Focus

Mental focus is also known as concentration, attention, or mind-set. When playing volleyball, the game action and the ball are moving so rapidly that even a split second of broken concentration can cost your team a game or the match. In order to maintain the proper mental focus throughout the match, several strategies may be used. First, you must learn to clear your mind of all irrelevant and distracting thoughts. This includes fan heckling, scouts, friends, or parents in the stands, how you did at school or work during the day, the error you made during the previous rally, and so forth. Second, since volleyball offers the perfect opportunity to refocus and regroup following a point or side-out, players should utilize this time wisely. The use of cue words or triggers (verbal or nonverbal) and pre-serve routines may be used to aid in maintaining proper focus or concentration. For example, you should have a consistent routine during this time from which you never deviate. Perhaps you talk to yourself, or slap the floor, or do whatever gets you into the right frame of mind to optimally perform during the next rally.

Visualization

The use of visualization and other forms of imagery can be very effective complementary strategies for beginning volleyball players. When learning any new skill, players must be able to form a mental blueprint of the actions and techniques necessary to successfully perform the skill. Since practice is the only way to improve, players will *physically* practice for hours, but rarely, if ever, will they mentally practice. Using visualization, players can mentally see themselves performing difficult skills correctly, which not only helps to build an effective mental blueprint, but also improves confidence in their ability to perform the skills. Because the mind and the body are intimately connected, the body will gradually begin to perform the skills as visualized in the head. Furthermore, you can trick yourself, since the mind is not capable of recognizing whether you are actually performing the skill physically or merely experiencing it in your mind! The images that you produce mentally actually send electrical impulses to the muscles involved in the activity or skill you are imagining, even though such movement is undetectable by the eye. Although visualization can be used at any time, the rest period between games and the short time between serves are ideal instances in which to use this strategy. The more "real" the imagined skill or activity is in your mind, the more effective the visualization. Thus, be certain that you are visualizing in color and that you see everything you would typically see in practice or in competition.

Self-Confidence and Goal Setting

As mentioned earlier, proper mental focus and the use of visualization can lead to enhanced levels of self-confidence. Goal setting is another strategy that is commonly employed to improve one's confidence levels. Self-confidence is the *single most vital aspect* of successful sport performance. No other psychological skill even comes close. So how does goal setting factor into this equation? First, goals direct the athlete's attention to skills needing practice and improvement. Second, goals mobilize the athlete's energy level and increase the amount of effort and persistence he or she will exert, particularly when improvement is slow. Finally, goals motivate athletes to search for new strategies to achieve those goals. In short, when goals are met through hard work, the player experiences success, which translates into improvement in self-confidence, which leads to better performance, which leads to more confidence . . .

Anxiety and Stress Management

In any sport and at any level, players invariably experience some degree of anxiety or stress. In general, anxiety has a negative effect on performance and must, therefore, be dealt with immediately and effectively if success is to occur. Anxiety may be mental (e.g., worry, self-doubt, etc.), physical (e.g., "butterflies" in stomach, rapid heartbeat, sweaty palms, etc.), or both, and is negative in several ways. First, it takes away from one's mental focus by serving as a distractor before or during performance. Second, increases in anxiety in the form of worry and self-doubt are generally associated with reductions in self-confidence. Finally, anxiety can directly influence performance, such as when a server who is experiencing a high level of anxiety serves the ball far beyond the parameters of the court. We know anxiety is generally bad, but the question is, what can we do about it?

Perhaps the best way a player can manage anxiety is to learn how to relax mentally and physically. As we mentioned earlier, the mind and the body are intimately connected—if you relax one, you will most likely succeed in relaxing the other. Thus, athletes must be able to talk to themselves in order to alleviate the anxiety (which is particularly difficult for beginners) or learn to physically relax themselves by using strategies such as progressive relaxation. Progressive relaxation is a technique that focuses on the major muscle groups of the body and involves tensing and relaxing each of these groups one at a time. This form of relaxation is commonly used prior to visualization (outside of competition or practice) and is very effective in relaxing both the mind and body while establishing a deep and calm breathing pattern. Being relaxed, however, does not imply that the player should feel sleepy and unalert. Rather, the body and mind must be aware and responsive. Players should spend approximately 15 seconds per muscle group before moving to the next one.

OFFENSIVE STRATEGIES

The most basic strategy in volleyball is to keep the ball in play one contact or hit longer than your opponent's team. To do this effectively, players must work together offensively to place the ball in a location or hit the ball with enough force to the opponent's side of the court that they are unable to return it back over. As we will discuss in the next section, "Defensive Strategies," players must also work together defensively so that the opponent's offensive attacks are blocked.

The best way to maximize a team's offensive ability is to utilize a successful pass-set-spike sequence. This makes it hard for the opponent's team to return the ball back over the net and increases the likelihood of scoring points. There are five general factors to consider when utilizing an offensive strategy (1) player specialization, (2) service reception, (3) attack formation, (4) attack coverage, and (5) free-ball coverage.

Player Specialization

It is our belief that all players in a physical education setting should become proficient and be able to successfully engage in all skills during a volleyball game. However, we realize that specialization is extremely important as volleyball game strategies are utilized. **Specialization** refers to training and utilizing individual players for one or two particular skills (i.e., setting or spiking) rather than training all players for all skills. Underlying the specialization concept is the assumption that the fewer functions an individual player has to learn, the greater the chance the player will become more proficient in performing those functions. In addition, specializing also helps identify player's functions during any offensive activity. Thus, it helps to create highly organized patterns of play. Players generally specialize as spiker/passers or setters.

specialization training and utilizing individual players for one or two particular skills (i.e., setting or spiking)

Service Reception

Service reception has to do with how a team receives a serve to best allow for a successful pass-set-spike sequence. Until a ball is contacted on the serve, both teams must be aligned on the court in their rotational positions. However, once the ball is contacted on the serve, players can move anywhere on the court and perform almost any skill. The exception is that only forward or front-row players can either spike or block in front of the attack line. The key to any effective service reception is that it provides for maximum court coverage. The easiest and most widely used service reception is the 5-player or W formation (see Figure 4.1). This formation allows for five players to be positioned to receive the serve. Notice that all areas of the court are covered. The right and left back positions

service reception how a team aligns itself to maximize the completion of a successful pass–set–spike sequence

Figure 4.1

"W" formation for service reception.

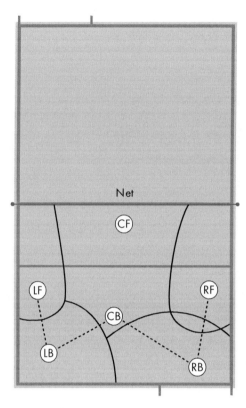

LF = Left forward   LB = Left back
CF = Center forward   CB = Center back
RF = Right forward   RB = Right back

cover the deepest part of the court whereas the left and right forward players cover the sides. The center back player covers the center-short area of the court. The sixth player (e.g., center forward) would be a specialized setter. Since the setter makes the second hit, he or she would not want to contact the ball from the serve. Thus, this player *always* positions himself or herself out of the way at the net or behind another player.

Attack Formations

Attack formations help to create very organized and specialized patterns of play and are usually described numerically. The first number refers to the number of players who serve as spikers. The second number refers to the number of players serving as specialized setters. Generally, the number of capable spikers is always higher than setters.

4–2 Attack Formation

The most basic attack formation utilized is the 4–2. In this formation, four players primarily serve as spikers while two players are designated setters. Since there are two designated setters in this formation, it is recommended that they be positioned opposite one another in the serving rotational order. Thus, one of the setters will always be in the front row. Initially, the setters should be positioned at the center forward and center back positions. This is the ideal position for the front-row or forward setter as it allows the player to set to either spiker in the left front or right front positions. If the front-row setter is rotationally positioned at either the left

Figure 4.2
The 4–2 attack formation.

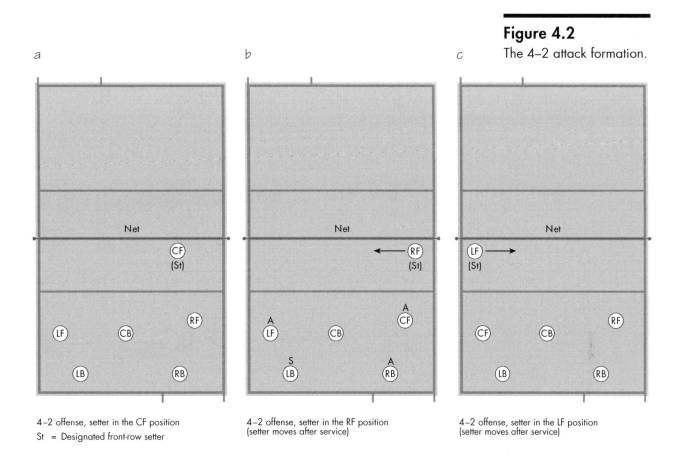

4–2 offense, setter in the CF position
St = Designated front-row setter

4–2 offense, setter in the RF position
(setter moves after service)

4–2 offense, setter in the LF position
(setter moves after service)

front or right front positions, he or she should always move to the center forward area after the service to be able to set the ball to teammates who would then be in either the left front or right front positions (see Figure 4.2).

4–2 International Attack Formation

The 4–2 international attack formation, like the traditional 4–2, has four designated attackers and two setters. The main difference is that the front-row setter is positioned in the right front area instead of the center forward area of the court. This change allows for spiking attempts to occur at both the center forward and left forward positions (see Figure 4.3). It also creates confusion on the part of the opponent's team since the setter is facing both possible spikers. Thus, the spike is not as easily telegraphed. Opponents who utilize the traditional 4–2 might also be at a disadvantage against a team utilizing the international formation, as their setter would be in the center forward part of the court. Since setters are generally the smaller players on a team, they might be at a height disadvantage in blocking against a designated spiker.

6–2 Attack Formation

As the name implies, the 6–2 formation has all players designated as attackers with two of those players also designated setters. Since this formation utilizes the setter from the back row or court area, it enhances spiking possibilities from all three front court positions. The setter can direct the ball to any forward position he or she chooses. The key is to get the designated setter into the frontcourt area before the served ball crosses the net (see Figure 4.4).

Figure 4.3

The 4–2 international attack formation.

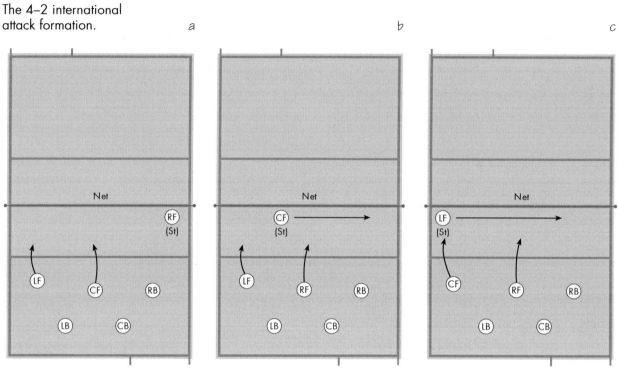

St = Designated front-row setter

Figure 4.4

6–2 attack formation.

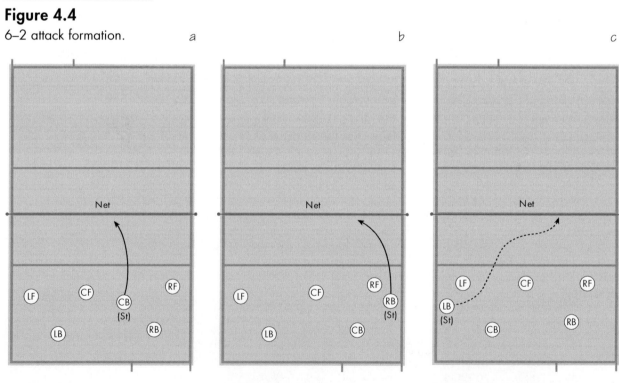

6–2 offense, setter in the CB position
(setter moves after service)

6–2 offense, setter in the RB position
(setter moves after service)

6–2 offense, setter in the LB position
(setter moves after service)

St=Designated front-row setter

Attack Coverage

After a team has used one of the attack formations discussed previously and initiated a successful pass-set-spike sequence, it is the responsibility of the offensive team to provide **attack coverage.** In other words, the offensive team needs to take steps to ensure that the ball could be played again in the event a spike happened to get blocked back onto the spiker's side of the court. The most basic coverage of the spiker is what is referred to as the 3–2 or circle coverage. The closest three players form a semicircle around the spiker while the other two players (i.e., farthest players) form a secondary semicircle. See Figures 4.5 to 4.7 for examples of different 3–2 spiking coverages based on the 4–2, 4–2 international, and 6–2 attack formations.

attack coverage *offensive player movement that ensures that a spiked ball could be played again in the event it is blocked back onto the spiker's side of the court.*

Free-Ball Coverage

There are times when a team cannot convert a successful pass-set-spike sequence. The players simply hit the ball back over the net to the opponent's side of the court (called a **free-ball**). This most often occurs when one of the first two hits (i.e., pass or set) were performed poorly. Thus, the last contact is meant to simply keep the ball in play. Obviously, a free-ball can be advantageous for the team receiving it as it "frees" them from blocking responsibilities and allows them to convert their own pass-set-spike sequence. The key is to recognize that a free-ball situation is occurring and move into position to set up an appropriate attack formation. Free-ball coverage is very much like serve reception coverage. The designated setter will move, if needed, to the front position on the court to be ready to make the second contact. The other forward players will move back to the attack line to initiate the spike (see Figure 4.8 for examples of movement patterns to set up the 4–2, 4–2 international, and 6–2 attack formations).

free-ball *ball that is hit over the net to opponents from a failed offensive attack*

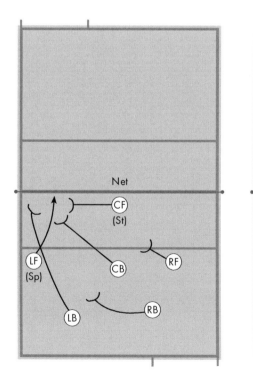

4–2 spike coverage when LF is spiking   *a*

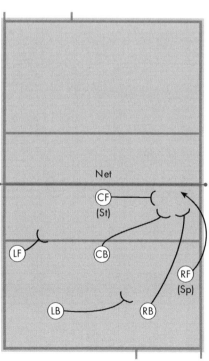

4–2 spike coverage when RF is spiking   *b*

St = Designated front-row setter

Sp = Spiker

Figure 4.5
3–2 spiking coverage for 4–2 attack formation.

Figure 4.6

3–2 spiking coverage for
4–2 international attack
formation.

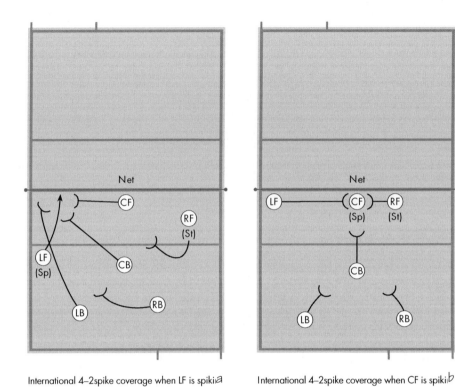

International 4–2 spike coverage when LF is spiking *a*

St = Designated front-row setter

Sp = Spiker

International 4–2 spike coverage when CF is spiking *b*

Figure 4.7

3–2 spiking coverage for
6–2 attack formation.

a *b* *c*

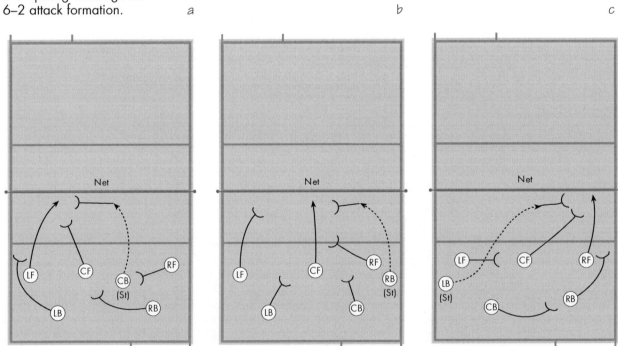

6–2 offense spike coverage when LF is spiking

6–2 offense spike coverage when CF is spiking

6–2 offense spike coverage when RF is spiking

St = Designated front-row setter

S t = Designated front-row setter

☆ = Wait till ball crosses net to initiate spike.

a   b   c

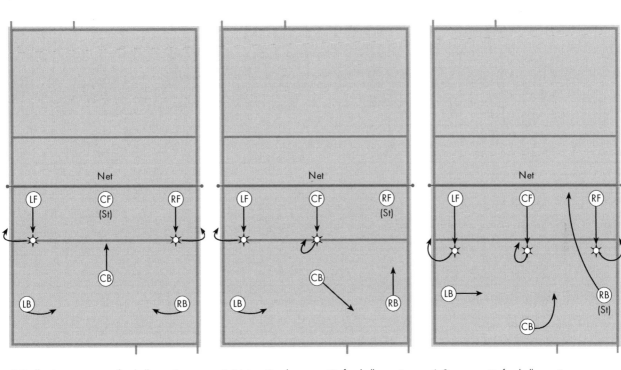

Figure 4.8

Movement patterns to set up the 4–2, 4–2 international, and 6–2 attack formations.

4–2 offensive movement to free-ball reception   4–2 international movement to free-ball reception   6–2 movement to free-ball reception

DEFENSIVE STRATEGIES

Defense is extremely important as it not only can help a team stop an opponent from scoring, it can help a team score itself. The primary purpose of any volleyball defense is to block the opposing team's spike and provide for court coverage. Obviously, the block responds directly to the opponent's spike whereas the court coverage responds to a spike that has gone through the blockers, a blocked ball that has traveled over the net, or a ball that has been dinked over the blockers. There are two general factors to consider when utilizing any defensive strategy: (1) player communication and (2) defensive formation.

Communication

It is imperative that players talk to one another about where the ball is heading and who is blocking the ball. Players need to call the ball when necessary and let each other know whether a ball is "free" or to be spiked by the opposing team. Words like "I've got it," "you take it," and "free-ball" should be heard continuously. Every member of a team should be involved in moving and communicating to those around them. Once a player has called for a ball, he or she should continue to play it unless called off by a teammate. Players near the sideline should call whether a ball will land "in" while back-row players need to determine and communicate whether a ball will be hit long.

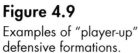

Figure 4.9

Examples of "player-up" defensive formations.

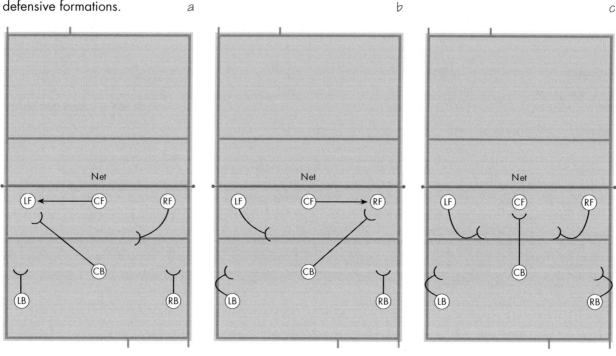

Blocking an attack by the opposing RF
St = Designated front-row setter

Blocking an attack by the opposing LF

Blocking an attack by the opposing CF

Defensive Formation

The easiest defensive arrangement to use is a "player-up" or 2–1–3 formation. In this defensive formation, two of the front-row players serve as the blockers. This would include the center forward and either the right or left forward depending on what side of the court the spike will be initiated from. One back-row player is always assigned to move up behind the block. This helps to cover for any dinks or mishits that happen to get behind the blockers. This person could be any back-row player, but for the purposes of player specialization, it is desirable that one pair of players positioned diagonally opposite in the alignment share the job. Thus, one of these players will always know to back up the blockers when they are positioned in the back row.

The opposite front-row player moves back to the attack line and plays balls that come off the block sharply or that come down the net to the inside of the court. The remaining two backcourt players position themselves so that they can play any balls hit through the block. The backcourt player nearest the spike should be able to play down-the-line spikes whereas the opposite backcourt player should be able to play crosscourt spikes (see Figure 4.9 for examples of "player-up" defensive formations for right, middle, or left side attacks). Notice that when an opposing team attacks from the center forward position, only a single block is initiated. The reasoning is that most center forward attacks are very quick and leave the outside forward players unable to help out.

SPECIFIC SKILL STRATEGIES

Volleyball involves the execution of skills and thinking about how these skills will be used in the context of the game. The following strategies should be considered prior to actually using these skills in the game.

Serving

The first objective of serving is to get the ball into the opponent's court. Once a player can do this consistently, he or she can then try to make it more difficult for the opponent to handle. The key is to serve to the weakest receiver on the team or to any area on the court that is hard to defend. Servers should try to serve the ball just over the net if the receiving team lines up far back in the court. The ball should be served deep if players are lined up close to the net. If the server notices that a team switches into a predetermined attack formation, he or she should serve the ball into players that might be switching positions. This can be effective because the players may switch too soon, or if they play the ball, the switch will be delayed. A team with a particularly skilled spiker should be served in a way that will make it difficult for them to get the ball to that spiker. For example, the ball could be served to the opposite side of the court (away from the spiker). Serves should also be generally varied among fast, slow, and floating. This makes it hard for the receiving team to key in on any one serve.

Defending the Serve

The receiving team should always place themselves in a receiving formation. Thus, each player's duties are known to the others. However, if a teammate is having problems returning a serve, other players can cover as needed. If another team starts to quickly score a few points off of the serve, the receiving team should call a time-out to regroup. Receiving players also need to remember to wait to see where the ball is going before they initiate a switch of positioning.

Forearm Passing

Most received balls should be played to the center front area of the court so that a team's setter can easily get under the ball to make a clean set. Thus, it is imperative that the first contact be directed to this location. Backcourt players, particularly, have to move to meet the ball. The ball should be called before contact. Also, whenever a player moves to a ball, he or she should play it. If this is not done, teammates might be faked out and the ball will not be played at all.

Setting

Most received balls should be played to the center front of the court so that a team's setter can easily get under the ball to make a clean set. If the setter is moving from the backcourt to the frontcourt, as in a 6–2 attack formation, he or she should hide behind the center forward position before the serve to avoid creating confusion on the part of the other back-row players. The setter should generally try to place the ball high above and approximately 2 feet back from the net, and close to the side boundary. He or she should also set the ball to the area where the weakest blockers are situated.

Spiking

A good spiker can hit over, through, and around the block. The key is to not be intimidated. The spiker should always be looking for holes in a defense. Placement is as important, if not more so, than simple power for effective spiking. Dinking the ball can be particularly useful is the spiker finds that the opponent's team does not effectively cover the court, particularly behind the blockers.

Blocking

Games are won by good blocking and court coverage. Having a blocker in a spiker's way creates, at the very least, a distraction for the spiker. It is important that every spike attempt be contested. The block should always be formed to take away the spiker's most consistent hit. If this is not known, take away the spiker's ability to hit the ball straight down the sideline. If a team has a particularly effective spiker, a double block should be consistently used. Also, never allow a spiker to hit through a hole between blockers.

SUMMARY

Overall, the effective use of strategies requires a realistic assessment of an individual team's abilities and limitations. A team that does not communicate well on the court is not going to be able to utilize more complicated offensive attack formations like the 6–2. In addition, players that have little experience or skill level will find it hard to incorporate strategies at all. This is why the use of strategies must be thought of developmentally. In other words, players need to be provided opportunities to practice simple strategies in drills and modified games before being expected to use them in the "real" 6-on-6 game. Allowing players to walk through offensive and defensive formations without having to perform the skills should take place prior to incorporating new strategies in actual drills and gameplay. Individual skill strategies (e.g., spiking around a blocker) should also be taught and practiced in various drill and modified game contexts prior to performing them in a game. Thus, the more game-like and strategic the drills during the learning process, the better able players will be to utilize strategies successfully in the game.

Glossary

aerobic exercise A form of training/conditioning that utilizes oxygen in order to produce energy needed for long-duration activity

anaerobic exercise A form of training/conditioning that does not require oxygen utilization to produce energy needed for short-duration bursts of activity

attack An offensive action intended to end play by hitting the ball to the floor on the opposing team's side of the court

attack coverage Offensive player movement that ensures that a spiked ball could be played again in the event it is blocked back onto the spiker's side of the court

attack line A line on the court parallel to the net and located 9 feet 10 inches from either side of the centerline; backcourt players must begin any attack from behind this line

block Defensive skill that involves intercepting the ball from an opponent's contact near the net

Federation Internationale de Volleyball (FIVB) Governing body for amateur international volleyball

footwork Ability to move forward, backward, and laterally with ease.

forearm pass Used to contact any ball below waist level (i.e., from a spike, the net, a block, or another

forearm pass) with the forearms in an underhand manner

free-ball Ball that is hit over the net to opponents from a failed offensive attack

interval training A conditioning program that trains both the aerobic and anaerobic energy systems by utilizing a pattern of work and rest intervals

kill A spike that cannot be returned

mintonette Original name of the game known as volleyball

rally The action initiated with the serve and ending with a point or side-out

rally scoring A method of scoring in which a point is awarded when either the serving or receiving team wins the rally

range of motion Flexibility/mobility of a joint

ready position an anticipatory position that will allow players to move quickly in any direction

rotation Clockwise movement of players on the serving team just prior to a serve and immediately following a side-out

serve Skill that puts the ball in play, representing the only time that your team can earn points in an official game

service reception How a team aligns itself to maximize service reception

set or overhead pass Used to contact any ball that is higher than shoulder level with the fingers and hands in an overhead manner

side-out The result of the receiving team winning a rally; no points are scored

specialization Training and utilizing individual players for one or two particular skills (i.e., setting or spiking)

spike Skill that involves hitting the ball hard and downward over the net into the opponent's court at a sharp angle

United States of America Volleyball Association (USAV) Governing body for the sport of volleyball in the United States

Index